Christian Commitment and Prophetic Living

Christian Commitment and Prophetic Living

Jeffrey G. Sobosan

CHRISTIAN COMMITMENT & PROPHETIC LIVING

© 1983 by XXV Publications. All rights reserved. No part of this publication may be reproduced in any manner without written permission of the publisher. Write to Permissions Editor.

ISBN 0-89622-291-1

Library of Congress Catalog Card Number 83-70100

Edited and designed by John G. van Bemmel.

TWENTY-THIRD PUBLICATIONS
Mystic, Connecticut

ISBN 9-89622-291-8
Library of Congress Catalog Card Number 85-52139

Edited and designed by John G. van Bemmel
Cover by George Herrick

"Jesus was a prophet. More than an ordinary prophet, he was **the** prophet, and the gospels show how he fulfilled his prophetic mission. Jeffrey Sobosan's work is about following Christ in his prophetic mission today. How is the prophetic call heard in the twentieth century? How is it lived? What spiritual difficulties should the prophet expect? And how can the prophet best deal with these? Sobosan has provided a practical spirituality for prophets, for men and women who have accepted the call to follow Christ in his prophetic mission. I doubt that anyone has ever tried to put together a spirituality for people engaged in the church's prophetic mission. Sobosan certainly fills a need, and he fills it well."

Eugene LaVerdiere, SSS
Editor, *Emmanuel* Magazine

"Jeffrey Sobosan has produced a very insightful book. Challenging and well phrased questions at the end of each chapter invite the individual or a group to pursue these insights and to let their consequences come home. This is one of those books that can really change the reader's life."

M. Basil Pennington, OCSO

"This meditation upon prophecy as an aspect of the Christian vocation is both disconcerting and provocative, and will be useful as an examination of conscience for religious activists. Fr. Sobosan offers a highly personal and imaginative composite profile of the biblical prophet, with parallels drawn to contemporary human affairs. Sobosan's insights will prune the *hubris* of those who would be prophets today, while also slicing away the excuses of those who would **not**. The book confronts the reader with issues that anyone who is serious about the Christian vocation must not avoid. Warning: To be read only when you have time to think and space to change your ways."

Marianne Sawicki
Lexington Theological Seminary

For showing me the meaning of loyalty
and the wondrous grace of a compassionate mind,
this book is for Tom, whom I love.

Preface

T he prophets initially played a very small part in my adult life, but with time they have come to play a major role. At first my interest in them was limited to the need for studying Scripture that was required during my training for the ministry, and later during my doctoral studies in theology. Then my interest became more extended as I started teaching at the university and was asked (simply because everyone else was either unavailable or uninterested) to teach a course on prophetic spirituality. While preparing this course, and then actually teaching it, I became aware of the influence the prophets were beginning to exercise over my own spirituality, and my growing conviction regarding their ingredient place in any Christian spirituality. It is this conviction that motivated me to write this book.

I could have proceeded along very scholarly lines, pursuing a book that would have been dominated by exegetical precision and detail, and proportionately requiring the reader's attentiveness and education. While I would be able, if asked, to justify my interpretations with much precision and detail, I have decided instead to avoid this type of scholarly exegesis. My reason is two-fold. First, there already exists an enormous number of such studies for the enlivened reader to examine. I can think offhand of the volumes I myself studied by Gerhard von Rad, Martin Buber, Abraham Heschel, R. E. Clements, H. M. Orlinsky, Claus Westerman, and many, many more. But second, and more importantly, my task in this book simply does not presume in the reader an interest avid enough to pursue this kind of in-depth study. Rather, it is more an exhortative or beckoning than an exegetical task I have set for myself. I am not taking for granted in the reader a familiar appreciation of the prophets or prophetic living. I am asking him and her to develop one, or at least to consider it.

It is not possible to discuss or analyze all the elements of a love affair, the way we might the elements of a complex theorem in geometry. There will always be something missing in the discussion, something absent in the analysis that leads us finally to say, "I know I am in love, but I just can't put all the reasons into words." This inarticulate dimension to love is what we call its mystery. For myself, I will say that the prophets who initially played a small part in my life, then an increasingly important one, have finally become my partners in a love affair. But what this means is that I will never be able to put into words all that this love involves. There will be experiences, insights, feelings that I do not describe even to my own satisfaction or that I fail to mention altogether. The reader should keep that in mind. Some may find gaps in my discussion, too much emphasis on some points, too little on others, approaches that shouldn't be taken, or taken with greater discretion. For example, while I will be much concerned with the place of hope in prophetic living, I will not take up the specifics of this hope in the teaching of biblical prophets on the coming of the "day" when divine judgment will complete the course of human development. This specific teaching I simply did not find useful for the spirituality I want to describe in this book. To my way of thinking, however, what these and similar observations would indicate is not antagonism but that the reader has also begun to love the prophets, and that our task is now one of mutual aid, so that our joint efforts to understand them better will make our common esteem more worthy.

There were many influences on me while composing this book. Aside from scholars such as those mentioned above, there have been colleagues, friends, students, admirers of my other books, and critics too, and many, many more — to all of them my debt is inexpressible. But the fundamental influence has been the prophets themselves. They have consoled and disturbed, enlightened and frustrated, lured and challenged me through all the pages that follow. They have been the devil's advocates to some of my most cherished prejudices, and won their case. They have been Socratic inquirers who highlighted the ignorance and insufficiency in some of my strongest convictions. They have been teachers who instructed me in a more thorough and grateful knowledge of the greatest of their number, Jesus — the one who manifested more clearly than all that prophetic living means nothing if the prophet is not also a servant.

Finally, let me make two further points before I close this preface. First, I will be using the word "prophet(s)" to mean both men and women. This will become immediately clear in my use of inclusive language when describing a prophet or prophets in general as opposed to a particular male or female prophet. On the other hand, I have also chosen to abide by the exclusive metaphor Jesus uses for God ("Abba") and so when speaking of God I will use masculine referents — all the while acknowledging that this is just a *metaphorical* preference. Secondly, much of the analysis in this book is creative. By this I mean that on a variety of points I have created a composite portrait of what a prophet is or does, which (at least biblically) may find explicit expression in only one or two, but certainly not all, of the prophets. In this task, needless to say, I have allowed my imagination full rein in order to make the analysis as relevant as I could to a contemporary Christian spirituality.

Jeffrey G. Sobosan
University of Portland
Portland, Oregon

Acknowledgments

A small amount of material (revised for inclusion in this book) has previously appeared in journals. I would like to thank the editors of these journals for permission to use this material: *The Journal of Religion and Health* for material in Chapters One and Six; *The Journal of the Interdenominational Theological Center* for material in Chapter Three; *The Journal of Psychology and Theology* for material in Chapter Four; and *Emmanuel* (19 E. 76th St., New York NY 10021) for material in Chapter Six.

I also wish to take this opportunity to thank Rev. Thomas E. Hosinski, C.S.C., for his constant humor and encouragement during long working hours. This book is gratefully dedicated to him.

Contents

Christian Commitment and Prophetic Living

For our God is a devouring fire.

Hebrews 12:29

CHAPTER ONE

Traditional Characteristics of Prophetic Living

To discover what the prophetic life involves means going to the prophets of the Old and New Testaments, the foremost of whom, from a Christian perspective, is obviously Jesus. In doing so one discovers that there are a number of traits to the prophetic life that are more or less pertinent to prophecy as a cross-cultural phenomenon: wonderworking, giving counsel, telling the future, and experiencing states of rapture or ecstasy. There are also some that are more or less related only to prophecy as it emerges in the two Testaments: the call, the authority, the criticism, the political involvement, and the reluctance. What I would like to do in this book is to concentrate on these five latter traits, since they indicate more clearly than the other four what I mean when I say that Christian living should enjoy a prophetic character. This does not imply, of

1

course, that the first four possess no value for Christian living. In fact, the intent of this chapter is to reflect briefly on ways to understand and appreciate them. But for the rest of the book I would like to avoid explicit discussion of these shared traits except when they relate to those five which I think are more directly pertinent to Christian living, if we agree that Christian living must be prophetic in character.

WONDERWORKING

Human beings love the spectacular. We are enthralled by experiences that exceed the ones populating our everyday lives, by talents that break our humdrum ordinary expectations, by power that controls the "natural" course of events. The spectacular opens up to us a world beyond the commonplace in which we usually dwell. It lets us know that the limits we set to human experiences, talents, and power are not as confining as they may first appear; that they can be broken. Yet because we often cannot (or will not) attribute this breaking of limits to human intervention, we attribute it to the intervention of the one whose experiences, talents, and power we can continually assert is superior to our own, to God. The logic here may sound naive to the educated reader; and in many of its applications it undoubtedly is. But if we take the prophets seriously, we must say that while this logic may often be naively applied, it is nonetheless workable as an explanation of the cause that breaks the limits which we think confine our lives.

For the prophet, in other words, this logic is no mere expediency, a handy "tool" for explaining what we cannot yet explain by other means. The prophet is not subject to the modern conceit that sees the activity of God as a stop-gap explanation for events which, with the progress of human knowledge, will eventually be replaced by the more reliable (and controllable) explanations of science and technology. For the prophet, God is not a convenience for human thought, an imaginary concept to be employed in discovering a yet unknown factor in our experiences, like the factor 'x' in geometric equations. No, the prophetic stance is clear and unambiguous: God is a free and autonomous being whom *we* don't employ but who employs *us* and whatever other means he chooses in working out his will in creation. The task of reflection is not to determine the limits of God's activity in our lives but the proper responses to his presence among us.

Faced with the prophetic trait of wonderworking, therefore, we usually find ourselves in a double bind. On the one hand we are lured by the record of the prophets' spectacular deeds; on the other we are suspicious of the neglect in the record of the role of human or natural intervention in these deeds; they are all immediately assigned to the power of God. It is a Jekyl-Hyde situation in which our subjective assessment of prophetic wonderworking is at odds with our objective assessment. Part of us is deeply touched, for example, when we read how Elijah humiliated the priests of Jezabel by bringing down lightning from the skies. But part of us would also be more persuaded if the prophet had convinced the pagan queen of his claims by lucid, rational argument. One commentator re-marked that the only time he is uncomfortable with the prophets is when they serve as mediators for the supernatural power of God. Elijah's lightning, like the staff of Moses that divides the waters of the sea or Jesus' changing water into wine, displays in spectacular fashion the control God exercises over creation. But we also want to become convinced of this control through the disciplined musings of our mind and heart where the need for the spectacular is absent. While we recognize, in short, that one parent giving birth to our convictions may be some spectacular deed or event outside ourselves, we also recognize that this parent is not only unnecessary but never sufficient. For we know that our convictions are likewise born, *and can only survive* from within us, that is, when their parent is our attentive thought, prayer, and study.

What finally establishes our faith in God, we are saying, is an internal discourse whose conclusion is an assertion that our faith is informed, intelligent, and persuasive. External events, things that happen in the world around us in striking and effective ways that seem to speak of the presence of God, can initiate and accompany our movement toward this faith. But the movement can ultimately achieve its goal only on the basis of what happens not outside but within us. So important is this point that we will embellish it throughout the following chapters. It provides a fundamental motive for why we have chosen to describe the prophetic life as one of untempered feelings.

Although we must direct a discreet eye, then, at all the accounts of prophetic wonderworking, this does not mean that the result of our judgment will always be a refusal to recognize a direct intervention by God in human affairs. We cannot fall prey to the chronic temptation that proposes the existence of a creating God, and then simultaneously asserts that he is completely inactive and uninvolved in the development of his creation, specifically human development. This is to become ensnared in the trap of deism. No, the God who emerges from the Old and New Testaments is not an indifferent Olympian, self-isolated on the island of heaven. He is a caring God, a Father in the favorite description of Jesus, actively engaged in the history of his creatures and regularly intervening in that history to provide guidance and judgment.

From a Christian perspective, therefore, it shows an extraordinary amount of unjustified self-confidence to determine that this activity or intervention can occur only in certain ways. For if we say, as Jesus does, that with God all things are possible, then we must acknowledge that this intervention can occur not only in quiet, indirect ways but also in spectacular, direct, and unanticipated ways. Whatever the objective reference to his miracles may be, for example, especially the miracles of healing and raising the dead, there is little doubt that Jesus' disciples interpreted them as manifest and unexpected intrusions by God into the "natural" course of events.

Yet their lack of gullibility in formulating this interpretation also continually emerges throughout the accounts in such implied (sometimes openly stated) inquiries as, "How can this be that lepers are cured? How can this happen that the dead are raised?" The contemporary Christian who views Jesus' disciples as clownish or childish or just plain silly in their understanding of his miracles as direct interventions of God's power in human life does them a terrible injustice. There is nothing clownish or childish or silly about any of them. In fact, the records of the miracles amply indicate that if these attitudes exist anywhere, they exist within such a contemporary Christian.

By using the word "spectacular" in these remarks I am not confining myself to extraordinary manipulations of natural phenomena, as in the Elijah incident already cited or in some of the miracles of Jesus recorded in the gospels. I implied as much above when I mentioned as an example of the spectacular the exercise of certain talents that individuals possess. I know a Christian woman, for example, whose facility at healing the ill, especially the ill in mind, impresses me as nothing short of a type of wonderworking, nothing less than spectacular. And I know other Christians whose ability at bringing peace among people, reconciling their differences in just and noble ways, is again a type of wonderworking for me, spectacular in action and results. The reader could isolate similar examples out of his or her own experiences. What they would all have in common is the basis they provide for asserting that God is not only active in our lives but frequently employs the agency of human beings, prophetic human beings, in wonderfilled ways to express this activity. The ordinary, the commonplace, the deadeningly predictable are then dissolved in the awareness that our lives are also subject to the extraordinary, the uncommon, the unexpected. We recognize that humdrum human living, which feeds the idea that the tight confines of our existence cannot be broken, is in fact always susceptible to the spectacular event that proves this idea wrong. The rut into which our expectations have fallen, the way we have allowed our hopes and desires to be channeled along very narrow paths are all capable of opening out into new horizons whenever God works his wonders through human prophets.

GIVING COUNSEL

Just as the prophets of the Old and New Testaments share the trait of wonderworking with their counterparts from other cultures, so they also share the gift of giving counsel. The prophet is known for wisdom, for insight into human behaviour. In a contemporary idiom we would say that he or she is able to "cut through to the heart of the matter." Sometimes the prophet is perceived as having earned this ability; it is the result of education, experiences, age, prayer, and so on. Sometimes the prophet is perceived as having it by natural talent; he or she simply possesses an extraordinarily intuitive and insightful mind that shows little relationship to education, experiences, age, and so on. Sometimes, finally, this ability is understood to be a gift of God, a charism that emerges in the prophet's life independently of natural or acquired talents. In all cases, however, the ability is identified as something extraordinary, that is, not possessed by or accessible to the majority of men and women. The counsel of the prophet makes sense out of a maddeningly ridiculous or antagonistic world when, for all our wit, we cannot. It is able to clarify experiences whose only trait seems to be their idiocy, the behavior of human beings intent on proving our boundless capacity for mindlessness and brutality, the hopes and desires that drive us when the future stares us down with the blank expression of a corpse. The prophet in counsel gives meaning to the absurdities of life, light to the darkness of our thoughts and feelings. Or differently: The prophet is living proof that there is available to us a guide in this often frantic and confused mess we call existence, a harbor of sanity among the wild and frenzied insanities that accompany us through the years. Our task is to find this guide.

Of course, the recognition of our need for counsel is not necessarily confined to particular crisis points in our lives. In a more extended context we may acknowledge it for determining the direction that our life as a whole should take. In this situation the counsellor we have selected then becomes more like a teacher to us, and our relationship is more accurately described as discipleship. It is this relationship, for example, that clearly defines what occurs between Jesus and the apostles. They seek his counsel not first to resolve crises that have emerged in their lives but to provide them with *a way of life*, a perspective in which to shape the values guiding their behavior, the faith and hope they may nourish, the virtues they need in order to achieve worthiness before the eyes of God. The apostles are not counsellees of Jesus, in the sense of seeking his wisdom and insight only momentarily in their lives to provide help in thinking through a particular problem or question. Rather, they are the disciples of Jesus, seeking his wisdom and insight as a lasting rubric for how they should live.

The concern of the disciple, in other words, is always much larger than the specific or parenthetical crises that dot his or her existence. It is as large as life itself and the need to determine an overall method for approaching it. The very awesomeness of this task is what motivates the disciple toward the humility required in any awareness that one cannot "go it alone," and thus to seek partnership with a teacher. A counsellor can be a convenience in life, someone who assists you through trying or disorienting situations, and then is left behind. But when the counselor is also your teacher (and you are a disciple), then the counsellor is a necessity whose assistance is left behind only with peril to your way of life.

The point I am making is that prophetic counsel, whether momentarily or lastingly practiced, clearly requires not only the possession of certain talents but the willingness to enter into sympathetic understanding with others. Wisdom that cannot be applied to the specific cares of human beings is barren. Insights that bear no pertinence to the felt exigencies of life remain mere abstractions, dry skeletons without flesh and blood.

Again, Jesus is a paradigm here. Even the images and metaphors he uses in offering his counsel, let alone when he offers it directly without the use of such aids, demonstrate a receptivity to the particular circumstances of human lives that is amazing. The wisdom of Jesus is always fertile, productive; his insights always breathe with meaning. This is what struck the apostles and made them his disciples. And to this day the distillation of this counsel of Jesus, the New Testament, is still making and sustaining his disciples.

This effect, I think, is what St. Paul is also getting at, though somewhat obliquely, in his famous doctrine of *mimetai* or "imitation." Just as we can come to a sympathetic understanding of Jesus only as we relate to him mimetically (reproducing his life in our lives), so we can come to a sympathetic understanding of any human being only as we again try to reproduce his or her life — its cares and fears, hopes and loves — in our own. Upon this mimetic relationship the effectiveness of our counsel of others, like the effectiveness of Jesus' counsel, rests. Or differently said: The spirit of self-abandonment, which we will suggest throughout this book must pervade the prophet's life as a whole, finds specific expression in the practice of counselling others. For whenever you are imprisoned in your own life, unwilling or unable to forsake concentration on what you find there, you can offer little or nothing to the lives of others. Instead of giving to them, you discover that all you can do is take from them.

The integral role of sympathetic understanding in prophetic counsel also points up the limits that constrain this counsel. Prophets must remain aware that whenever they cannot sympathetically appraise the lives of other human beings, they must either refuse their counsel altogether or clearly add the cautionary note that it may not be worthy or relevant. Or, in an always wise and simple option, they may confine their counsel to the advice that someone else more qualified than they be approached.

What this particular characteristic of prophetic counsel is trying to avoid, in other words, is the arrogance whereby an individual begins to think that his or her viewpoint in any situation is always wise and insightful. The prophet is not subject to that strange logic whereby an individual thinks that because success is achieved in one situation (in our case the counselling of another) success will be achieved in all similar situations — like the expert scientist who, because of her expertise in science, thinks she is also an expert theologian. This is the logic, the arrogance of the "proud and haughty" judges whom Isaiah condemns. It is a direct offense against the humility, the awareness of limits that confines prophetic life from its very beginning, simply because the prophet as a human being is a limited and confined being. All of which finally means: The prophet is not a trickster, a manipulating "guru" who benefits whenever possible from the pain and confusion of others. Instead, every true prophet will confess that whatever value his or her counsel possesses must be willingly given to others, but that this value is something *they* (not the prophet) will proclaim once it has been applied in their lives.

TELLING THE FUTURE

Of all the traits characterizing the prophetic life, this is by far the most prominent in popular understanding. Language itself betrays this fact insofar as the phrase "to prophesy" has for most people become synonymous with the phrase "to tell the future." The untutored imagination, we are saying, pictures the prophet as basically a soothsayer, someone who by various forms of sorcery or magic is able to envision the course of events in the near or distant future. In its most corrupt form there finally emerges the image of the prophet as a "fortuneteller," an individual who (usually for a price) will read the stars, tea leaves, your palm, or a crystal ball to offer counsel on what you can anticipate in order to assist any present decisions you make.

Needless to say, with this extreme position we have departed alarmingly from the role the future plays in an authentic prophetic life. We are more in the world of circuses and cheap carnivals than in the world of the two Testaments. It is the world of all thoughtless men and women who, unable or unwilling to make choices for themselves or to exercise even the simplest foresight regarding the future of their lives, will run to any charlatan parading a desire or ability to assist them. It is the world of all manipulators who grow fat on the gullibility or mental indolence of others by convincing them that with the knowledge he or she can provide they can arrange their lives so as to avoid unhappiness, satisfy desires, gain whatever of wealth and fame they wish — in short, how they can be "saved." For these manipulators know that we are all susceptible to the curse Zeus laid upon humankind when his beautiful minion Pandora, opening her jar of woes, released on the world all the sufferings men and women know, yet not the one thing they now needed, the ability to anticipate the future (what the Greeks called *elpis*), especially future pain. The charlatan prophet claims that he or she has looked into Pandora's jar, sees what the future holds, and can tell you what you may expect in life, all by his or her own prowess. This is the false prophet who claims to be the healer of Zeus' curse.

It can be argued that regarding the question of time there are three fundamental stances an individual can take to shape a meaning for life. The first stance is what we could call the *aesthetic*. Here you concentrate on the present as the "place" from which you draw meaning. The criterion of your behaviour is the needs and desires you have now, with little or no attention to how these needs and desires influence your understanding of your past or future life. The literary paradigms are Don Juan and Lolita; a commonplace example would be the college student whose whole life seems to center on the party enjoyed last weekend or to be enjoyed this coming weekend.

The second stance is the *ethical*. Here you concentrate on the past as the place from which you draw meaning. The criterion for your behavior is captured in a phrase like, "This is what I (or we) have always done," and within its context you determine the worthiness of present decisions and future hopes. The literary paradigm is the Wandering Jew, the individual who, armed with the laws of Moses, can live in any place and at any time and know exactly what to do. A commonplace example would be the middle-age parents whose only standard of judgment on the behaviour of their children seems to be the complaint, "That isn't the way we acted when we were your age."

The third stance could be called the *religious*. Here you concentrate on the future as the place from which you draw meaning. The criterion of your behaviour is some goal or event ahead of you that retroactively influences the way you view your past and the current decisions you must make. The literary paradigm here is the prophet in the two Testaments. A commonplace example would be any individual whose hope for the future organizes present activity and judgment on the past. To live a prophetic life, in other words, is to exist within this religious stance. While neither ignoring or diminishing the importance of the past or present, the prophet recognizes that this importance is directly dependent on a vision of the future. When we read, therefore, of someone like Jeremiah or the woman Huldah trying to break down established ways of thinking and acting among their contemporaries, we know that it is because they believe God wants the community of Israel re-created, planted again and built up for a new future (cf. Jeremiah 31:1-8). The roots of the community remain the same; the soil is still that of the desert wilderness where Israel was faithful to Yahweh (Jeremiah 2:23). But Jeremiah and Huldah must show their contemporaries that if there is to be fidelity to the past, they (the contemporaries) cannot remain content with the present, which has been made inadequate by their choices. Which is to say: The prophet is a preacher of the future as the place where the past and present will find their eventual fulfillment in the presence of God. The prophet is not only the seer but also the critic of the people of God (as we will see in Chapter Four), the guide and conscience of the people as they fulfill their mission in journeying to their goal.

We have already made clear how ludicrous it is to think that in shaping a vision of the future the prophet relies on the carnival methods of the fortuneteller. The prophet is never willing to speak about the future at random; there is no trigger in his or her mind that unveils the whole panorama of coming events and allows a commentary on any or all of them. The prophet does not perform; the prophet *prophesies*, that is, preaches a vision of the future which is always circumscribed, channeled in a specific direction based on perceptions of the past and present. This is a particularly important point, since much contemporary use of the prophets (especially the Old Testament prophets) largely ignores it. Thus we have the uninformed preacher haranguing an audience into believing that the future envisioned by an Isaiah or Ezekiel can be understood and applied today without qualification. This not only represents what we just described as the ethical stance in shaping meaning for one's life; it represents as well a terrible injustice to the prophets themselves, who prophesied for their own generation and not a generation 2500 years in the future.

It is an assault on intelligence, if not an act of dishonesty, to take the words of others out of the context in which they were spoken and pretend that you are accurately assessing their meaning for the speaker. The most you can do in this situation, rather, is offer an interpretation of what the words mean to *you*. All of us, I am saying, are wise to remain aware of the fact that one of the oldest tricks in human argumentation is to present a personal opinion as if it were the viewpoint of a mutually recognized authority — especially when this authority is not available to confirm or deny how the viewpoint is being used. This is the ancient (sometimes infamous) *argumentum ex auctoritate*, which theologians especially seem very adept at employing. It always holds within it a proclivity toward the brute manipulation of others for the triumph of your personal opinion (whatever this might mean in a particular instance) rather than having to convince others of it through informed and relevant, persuasive and respectful discourse drawn from your own mind.

There are two fundamental sources from which the prophets develop their vision of the future. The first we have just implied in the paragraph above. On the basis of their knowledge of past and present situations, the prophets are able to offer an intelligent prediction of some future course of action. This is a talent, we may note, which the ancient Greeks especially cherished and which they called "forethought" (this, in fact, is the meaning of the name of one of their favorite godlike heroes, the titan Prometheus, as opposed to his brother Epimetheus, meaning "afterthought"). If you know, for example, that the Assyrians are led by an aggressive king, and if you know that their past indicates military prowess, and if you know that current data indicate a turning of attention toward your homeland — then anyone with the forethought of an Isaiah could reliably predict an *eventual* invasion by the Assyrians. The prophet does not need talismans, magical incantations, or the entrails of dead animals to see what the future predictably holds. In most cases the only thing needed is an informed and intelligent mind. And the fact that the prophet demonstrates just such a mind should permanently allay any misconception, however commonplace it might be, that he or she exists in a self-created world, isolated from reality while wrestling with the angels and demons that roam a disturbed spirit. The prophet does not seek to flee the world, no matter how repugnant it might be. Rather, the prophet seeks to become invested in it, struggling, fighting, playing with it so as to understand its past and present and guide with knowledgeable forethought its future.

The second source from which the prophets develop their vision of the future is more difficult to explain, since it involves the intrusion of a factor outside the circle of their own talents and intelligence. That factor is a revelation from God. There are two fundamental faith-assertions operative here, and we will return to them more than once in the following chapters. The first is that God is not aloof from creation, indifferent to the issue of human development. The second is that because of this involvement God periodically "intrudes" into human development to express his will via the mediation of select human beings. When the prophet structures a vision of the future, in other words, it is not *always* something generated out of the knowledge and insights of a creative mind; frequently the prophet perceives that this vision is something endowed by another, who is then identified as God. As we will see in the following chapters, it is this perception that will require us to consider its theological character as the pre-eminent context in which to understand prophetic life. It is the same perception that explains why the prophet will inevitably appear to the completely secular or profane mind as somewhat naive or deluded. For the profane or secular mind can assign God no role in human affairs except that of a playful fancy that either remains harmless or, when taken too seriously, turns sour and inhibiting for the practice of human freedom.

The future the prophet foretells, when this is cast within the context of a revelation from God, will always appear to the profane mind as a constraint upon the rightful dignity of human beings to establish and puruse their destinies as independent agents. The profane or secular mind is inerrantly bemused or frightened by the fact that the prophet is continually *theotropic,* "God-leaning" or "God-directed," in the existence he or she leads.

For some people the future is terrifying. The last thing they wish to do is structure a vision of what may lie ahead of them. This is typically an "echoing" effect of the unhappiness or joylessness of their past and present lives. They cannot imagine that the future will be any different from what life is or has been, and so they shun all thought about the future. They take naive if not happy consolation in a statement like that of Jesus, "Sufficient for today are its own troubles." In this state of mind the individual is closed off from the prophetic function of telling the future.

But we will argue in following pages that this is simultaneously a stricture on the responsibility required if indeed an individual is to lead a prophetic life. For the true prophet knows that the meaning of what we do cannot be successfully drawn from the present or the past but only from the future, the place where our goals reside and fidelity to the will of God, fidelity to our convictions regarding what we must do in life, is finally proved. Or to elaborate a critical point made just above: The past functions as a pedagogical tool, a training ground for self-knowledge. But it does so only in service to the present, the current contexts and situations in which we must make the decisions that shape our lives. Yet to this the prophet will at once add that the present, like the past, is also not an end in itself. *The self-knowledge we gain from the past and the decisions we make in the present achieve their worth only when they relate to the goals we have set for the future.* These goals, this future dominate prophetic consciousness. And because of this, telling the future, anticipating it with intelligence and faith, becomes a characteristic of prophetic living.

ECSTASY

If there is any trait of the prophetic life that runs a clear second in popular understanding to that of telling the future, it is the experience of ecstasy. To the untutored imagination the prophet is frequently pictured as an ecstatic "luminary" who hears voices, sees visions, and has available a myriad of wondrous experiences that most men and women do not. When this imagination turns sour the prophet becomes an eccentric who demonstrates schizoid behavior that has left the solid anchor of the "real world" behind in favor of an imagined one where there is easy converse with spirits and gods.

Neither of these descriptions, of course, like the popular one of prophetic future-telling, does justice to what prophetic ecstasy means.

Each favors what we described earlier as the human love for the spectacular. Only now the spectacular has become synonomous with the grotesque, and the word "prophet" begins to be defined in terms derived from mystagogic religion or psychopathy. This is the position of the "cultured despiser of religion" (to use Schleiermacher's term) for whom any account of prophetic ecstasy will always remain fundamentally a lie, a device to explain experiences whose truth must be explained by other means.

This is not necessarily an antagonistic judgment, openly scornful and contemptuous of the prophet. It is more likely to be one of pity, a saddened concern that the prophet has succumbed to the intrigues of a distorted imagination. Between the cultured despiser of religion and the prophet, therefore, a door must be opened for dialogue, a method of communication so that the despiser can speak to the prophet of the possible distortions of his experiences, and the prophet can speak to the despiser of the possible extensions of experience open to a receptive human mind. Otherwise there can only be two monologues between them, each representing the utter conviction of its position. And this situation, *whenever* it occurs in human relationships, obviously benefits no one except as it simply conveys information.

We have already noted that the driving force behind the prophetic life (at least as this is understood in the two Testaments) is the conviction that God's will is known. For the prophet this knowledge is gained in either one of two basic ways, each of which we've already implied in the previous section on telling the future. The first and by far more common of the two is what we might call the revelation "to the fathers" (in the Old Testament this will frequently mean Moses). What the prophet is asserting here is that history has not been derelict of God's spoken word but provides expressions of it which must be cherished. But this cherishing is not like the type we might direct toward some reliquary holding a precious object from the past. For then it could too easily become little more than an admiring but unproductive devotion. No, the prophets cherish the revelation of God's will to the "fathers" because it provides the framework within which they can build the criteria for their present behavior and, most importantly, the content of their vision of the future, their hope. Thus anyone reading the prophetic books of the Old Testament becomes immediately struck by their so-called conservatism, their repeated reference to past revelation.

This impression is valid, however, only when it is elaborated within the context of the above stance and not the "ethical" stance described above. The past, as we said, functions pedagogically for the prophet. It is the *first* concern, the first object of study and prayer and reflection. But it is only a tool for the prophet's *final* concern, which is the possibilities the future holds for the people of God.

The second way knowledge of God's will is gained is through ecstasy. The ecstatic rapture of the prophet is not dissimilar to what Abraham Maslow calls a "peak experience." It involves a concentration of the prophet's consciousness in a way that makes available experiences otherwise absent from everyday life. Three important points can be made about these experiences, at least if we confine ourselves to the prophets of the Old Testament. First, the experiences are almost always auditory, that is, the prophet becomes aware of an interior dialogue going on in which he or she is one partner and God is the other. Descriptions of this dialogue, however, will frequently externalize it so that God is actually portrayed as a distinct presence conversing with the prophet.

This leads to the second point, that the content of the ecstatic rapture, the message being delivered in the dialogue, has not been generated solely from the prophet's own mind — from personal hopes and fears, values and biases. The descriptions of the independent partnership of God in the dialogue are meant to prohibit the idea that the ecstatic experience can be explained simply by explaining the psychological or spiritual peculiarities of the prophet.

This in turn finally leads to the third point, which is that the ecstatic rapture (or at least the initial one experienced by the prophets in the Old Testament) is never portrayed as the product of personal discipline. The prophet has not followed a routine of rigid purgations designed to produce an ecstasy. Instead, the experience occurs in a way that causes a response from the prophet we might describe as surprise, or perhaps better, shock. Again, this third point is meant to indicate the autonomous role of God in the experience, and to offset the accusation that what is occurring during the prophet's ecstasy is occurring only as the result of a wayward imagination. We may note in passing that this particular trait of the prophetic

life will occupy us at much greater length in the next chapter while
discussing the specific experiences of the prophet's "call."

What all prophets are asserting, then, in their descriptions of
their ecstatic dialogue with God is not only that the past has not
been derelict of God's spoken word ("to the fathers") but that neither
has the present (to the prophets themselves). God speaks today just
as he did yesterday, and each time he speaks, his words must be
cherished in the way we described. In the biblical witness, in other
words, the prophetic trait of ecstasy, like the other three we have
named, must be understood primarily in a theological context. In
the wonders worked, in the counsel given, in the future envisioned,
and in the ecstasies experienced, the prophet is not alone but is
partnered with a God who reveals his will to a developing humanity.
Without an awareness of this theological context, or by refusing to
accept it, any understanding of prophetic life as it emerges in the
Old and New Testaments will produce a truncated appreciation of
a way of living that we will suggest throughout this book deserves
our full appreciation. The presence of God in prophetic life is like
the presence of the beating heart in a human body. Without it,
prophetic life dies.

We noted at the beginning of this chapter that the first four traits
of prophetic life find parallels in men and women outside the religious
matrix of the Bible. We can think, for example, of the seers of ancient
Greece, the magi of ancient Persia, or even the shamans in the tribal
societies of American Indians. These men and women likewise
worked wonders, gave counsel, told the future, and experienced
ecstasies. Yet, we also noted at the beginning of the chapter that there
are five other traits to prophetic life which, apart from these first
four, are more directly pertinent to all those who base their way
of living on the two Testaments — for Christians especially, the New
Testament witness to Jesus. These traits are our dominant concern
in this book, and to them I now turn in its remaining pages.

QUESTIONS FOR REFLECTION AND DISCUSSION

1. Would you be willing to argue the claim that God works "natural" or physical wonders in the world — for example, that God can cure what physicians cannot? Why? Why not?

2. How would you describe both the various ways people might need prophetic counsel in life, and the individuals to seek in securing this counsel?

3. Which of the prophetic understandings of time — what I called, following Kierkegaard, the "aesthetic," the "ethical," and the "religious" — does our culture (and our church) encourage in us?

4. If someone, experiencing prophetic ecstasy, said to a child, "I have heard the voice of God," the child might likely respond, "What did God say?" If the person said the same thing to you, how would you respond, and why would you respond in that way?

5. Of the four traits of prophetic living described in this chapter, which one, do you think, contemporary Christians in our culture need most?

CHAPTER TWO

The Call

When I was a child I had an imaginary playmate. I kept her a secret because I thought other people would ridicule me if I told them she existed. But in my solitude I would converse with her as if she really were another little child sitting or standing beside me. I remember that some of the most "serious" decisions I made as a child were formulated under the influence of her advice. I would call to her and she would call to me; I would laugh or cry with her, she would laugh or cry with me. There was no doubt whatever in my mind that she was clearly the best friend I would ever have.

As I grew older, of course, wiser in the judgment of others, I realized that my playmate wasn't real at all. She was an alter-ego, a companion structured out of my childhood needs and imaginings. The advance of years had brutalized one of the finest possessions I owned. The boundaries of its reality were invaded, many of its specific characteristics dismantled. Finally, when the whole process was complete, all I was left with was the voice. Everything else had faded or been dismissed from my consciousness. But the voice still remained. To this day it still calls, it still instructs, laughs, cries, and reprimands. It still speaks with untempered feelings.

The sayings of the mind and heart can remain a monologue. There is no discussion, no doubt or debate within you. There is no posing of options, no awareness that a different perspective might be taken on the way you look at things. In this situation the voice within always speaks with absolute judgment. Its mode is unremittingly the imperative, and you are its slave. No longer a playmate through life, it is now a tyrant whose will is without constraint. The voice speaks, but it speaks alone; your response is silence and submission. Your mind, in other words, is like a musical score in which your consciousness permits only one sound to be heard. Hence, the diversity required for harmony is absent and your thinking takes on the absoluteness (and reliability) of a steady hum, while lacking the creative interplay of sounds that is a prerequisite for all true music.

This type of dictatorial consciousness is demonic. It straps you into one way of thinking that immediately rebukes any refinement or contradiction. Any call to a different way of thinking, a changed way of looking at the events and situations that populate your life, is crushed into irrelevance or forgetfulness. The millionaire physician who works her craft only for the benefit of the wealthy, may someday hear a voice calling her to leave all that she has and give her curing talent to the poor. But the voice is gagged as soon as it speaks. For it has offended the tyranny of a consciousness that has grown large on the thought that her healing skills are simply handmaidens to her bank account. A consciousness that speaks with one voice can only engage in a monologue. Dialogue is possible only when more than one voice speaks, and each is respected for what it says.

A VOICE WITHIN:
THE EXPERIENCE OF VOCATION

The ancient theology that recognizes God's revelation of his will as principally verbal, a Word, is premised on the idea that more than one voice must speak within us. This, however, does not simultaneously require a type of schizophrenic "break" within us, a splitting of our personality into distinct, autonomous parts — as some psychologists of religion have unwisely (and often unfairly) suggested. What it requires, rather, is a willing acceptance of the idea that within every single personality, just as within every single work of music, there is a diversity of parts that must be respected if harmony, a sense of wholeness, is to be achieved. But like a work of music too, we may say that while God's will is a call, it is not compelling. We are not forced but invited to listen to it. We may ignore the invitation, of course, refusing the dialogue it would initiate within us. In this case our preference is unmistakably clear: We wish to guide our lives without any intrusion that would force the breaking of our monologue with ourselves, our settled ways of thinking and feeling. The beckoning call of God, the proposal that we hear what he has to say, that we speak with him, goes unheeded. Our hearing turns to deafness for the sake of comfort. For the call of God, we fear, can only bring disruption into the life we have planned. It is better for us to remain silent, unresponsive before it.

Or we can listen to the call; we can entertain it. The security of speaking only to ourselves, hearing only what we wish to hear, gives way to the excitement, the enchantment of speaking to another. We make no decisions yet as to the worthiness of what the other might say, but we will listen. If persuasive, we will concede to the persuasion; our ways of thinking and feeling will respect what we have heard. If unpersuasive, this too will be acknowledged; our ways of thinking and feeling will achieve greater justification. But we know that whatever the result may be, we must first *listen* to the other; that to refuse to listen is to paralyze ourselves, remaining neither changed nor strengthened in how we think and feel.

When you engage in conversation with a friend you respect, your attention to what is said will be much greater than it is when you are in conversation with someone you do not respect. You will be much more willing to let what you hear influence the way you think and feel. Or when you hear someone speak whose reputation for wisdom and insight is acclaimed, your attention again will be far more acute than it is when someone is speaking who does not have a similar reputation. Here too your willingness to allow the other's words to influence how you think and feel will be more keenly receptive. In each case what the other says will bring to life a voice within you that will begin its play, its dialogue, with how you presently think and feel.

In other words, just like the child's refusal to play with an unwanted or unadmired companion, you too will refuse to play with the voice within you if it also is unwanted or unadmired. You will show either an empty courtesy toward it or a condescending tolerance or a deaf indifference. Only if the voice becomes insistent, like the child's spurned playmate — if it gets louder, if it starts screaming — will you have to begin attending to it. For now it is not just an intrusion into your life but an inconvenience, an annoyance you must address. Perhaps this is one of several meanings we can attach to Jesus' parable of the widow (Luke 18:1-6). Her persistence before the king, the refusal to allow his indifference to defeat her pleading, eventually gains his attention. The king achieves peace of mind, the alleviation of the woman's cries calling to him, only when he decides to listen to what she is saying and grant it an influence over his judgments.

Sometimes God's voice within works in the ways I have just described; how it speaks depends on the receptiveness we grant it. When it is a recognized and respected voice it need only speak quietly to gain our attentiveness. Elijah's experience is a well-known illustration:

> The Lord was passing by: a great and strong wind came rending mountains and shattering rocks before him, but the Lord was not in the wind; and after the wind there was an earthquake, but the Lord was not in the earthquake; and after the earthquake fire, but the Lord was not in the fire; and after the fire a low murmuring sound. When Elijah heard it, he muffled his face in his cloak and went out and stood at the entrance of the cave. Then there came a voice: "Why are you here, Elijah?"

Elijah knows that the voice speaking to him is God's and that it need only speak softly to secure his attention. Moreover, the fact that the voice not only speaks but also wishes to initiate a dialogue with him is implied in the questioon posed at the end: Elijah is expected to respond to what is asked, as he does in the verses that follow. The prophet is thus demonstrating the first and fundamental characteristic of all prophetic living: *an experience of God's call that initiates an internal conversation that is persuasive and effective over the prophet's life.* (Classic records of this experience can also be found in Isaiah 6, Jeremiah 1, and Ezechiel 1-3. Even where there is no explicit record, however, some such experience seems implied in phrases like, "The word of the Lord came to . . . .") After speaking with God, the prophet cannot remain the same person. For a new reality, a new power has now come alive within the prophet that will henceforth determine all he or she does.

Sometimes, on the other hand, the voice of God needs to speak persistently, loudly, for our receptivity toward it is reluctant. We listen but are not listening closely. All the while the voice is speaking we are thinking of ways to contradict or diminish the importance of what is being said. We are settled in our lives, our ways of thinking and feeling, and we fear entertaining a conversation that might disrupt our contentment. And so God speaks forcefully to us now, knowing our hesistation. He no longer relates to us as he did to Elijah, in a soft, murmuring sound. He now relates to us as he did to the reluctant Moses on Sinai, in the forcefulness of an unconsuming fire.

The first of the prophets is unenthusiastic when he hears the call of his God. He is comfortable in his life as a shepherd, soothed by its domesticity, its predictability, the everyday love of his wife Zipporah. Yet God will not allow his voice to be ignored, nor what he says easily denied. The last place Moses wishes to go is back to Egypt, but God insists for the sake of his people. The last thing Moses wishes to do is preach a message of freedom — he is a poor speaker, words come slowly to him — but God vows the help of Aaron to make up the deficiency. To each of Moses' reasons for refusing the urgency of God's voice, the persuading partner in the dialogue increasingly becomes God. Moses finally relents, convinced that the voice of God must change his life. Put differently, we could say that what he is demonstrating is a maturity that recognizes that a point has been reached when all his excuses have run out. Then he knows that he can do either one of two things: He can continue to refuse the persuasiveness of his partner's words, trapped in a stubbornness that makes him an object of pity or contempt, or he can submit to his partner's words, as indeed Moses does, knowing that personal integrity offers no other choice. The cleverness of his excuse making, in short, gives way to the humility that respects even unpleasant convictions.

No one can force us to take what he or she says seriously. Our seriousness in listening is a decision we make on the basis of an anticipation of the worthiness of what we will hear. The anticipation may at first be a weak one, but as we continue to listen we become more attentive; the worthiness of what is being said is greater than we had thought. Or conversely, the anticipation may at first be a strong one, but as we continue to listen we become less attentive; the worthiness of what is being said is poorer than we had thought. Everyone has experienced each of these situations. They describe one of the defining characteristics of human relationships: The quality of our listening is directly related to our anticipation of what we will hear. And this anticipation, as we said earlier, will frequently be determined by our preliminary appraisal of the one speaking to us. This preliminary appraisal applies even when we believe it is the voice of God addressing us.

ENTHUSIASM AND DOUBT

Even the most truncated understanding of Christian faith will affirm at least this much: In the public ministry of Jesus, in his words and deeds, we have a revelation of God's will for us. In what Jesus said and did the voice of God is speaking to us, and the record of that voice, the New Testament, is a sustained call to engage in conversation with God. But how the call is greeted, whether with involved enthusiasm or mild interest, open disdain or indifference, will depend on our disposition toward the one calling. If God is like a flutter in your mind, for example, an idea that irregularly emerges into your consciousness, then you will likely possess only a mild, periodic interest in conversing with him, no matter how consistent the invitation to speak might be. Or if God is like an enemy in your mind, an opponent to be fought and defeated, then you will likely possess an antagonistic, denying attitude toward the call to speak with him. The battle lines have been drawn and there is nothing more to be said that can influence your viewpoint. Or if God is like an irritant in your mind, an inconvenience that you cure by ignoring it, then you will likely possess an indifferent, silent attitude toward his voice inviting you into conversation.

Only if God is like a respected companion in your mind, someone whose words elicit great anticipation from you, will you greet the call to conversation with involved enthusiasm. You will want to enter into God's words ("enthusiasm" from *en theos*, in or into God) in the hope that they will donate something new to how you think and feel. It is this attitude, this enthusiasm that is the pre-requisite before the voice of God calling in the words and deeds of Jesus will be heard with eager attentiveness.

We often try to temper our enthusiasm. We have been taught, for example, that enthusiasm is unseemly; that it indicates a lack of discretion, a certain ill-manneredness that might be tolerated in a child but is unbecoming in an adult. We therefore tighten the limits of our responsiveness because we believe it is the mature thing to do (*matur*, to prune or cut away). Or we are somewhat afraid of our enthusiasm. We suspect its hold over us, its alarming ability to lure from us activity that in calmer moments we would never per-form. In either case we prove ourselves reluctant to engage the untempered feeling that someone like Isaiah discloses when before the call of God to preach to the Israelites he responds, "Here I am, Lord. Send me!" Isaiah is not thinking of the unseemliness of his enthusiasm, the embarrassment it might subsequently cause him. And he is certainly not suspicious of it, fearing the authority it might exercise over his behaviour. When his God calls he knows nothing of a hesitation born from pride or fear. He makes his availability apparent without restraint. All that interests him are the words his God will now speak to him; all he wishes to do is listen and learn.

What Isaiah demonstrates, in other words, is the docility characteristic of every good student. There is an excitement in his response to God, a willingness to allow God's words to influence him that forbids the disrespect or indifference characteristic of every bad student. The conceit of the intellectual bully is absent in the prophet. The trembling of the frightened mind at being taught something new ("Please, I don't want to hear it!") finds no home in the prophet.

The steady activity of the mind, its eternal readiness to doubt and question everything, is frequently isolated as the foremost mark of human dignity. Because we can pose options to ourselves — because we can doubt, and in doubting free ourselves from singular, unthinking patterns of behavior — we believe we possess a nobility denied the rest of creation. But our felt pride in this ability, upon reflection, can become worrisome.

The worry centers precisely on the *steadiness* of our doubt, our willingness to question the legitimacy of any and all experiences we have, which in turn inevitably affects the enthusiasm with which we greet the experiences. We hold back from embracing them, the truth and meaning they seem to hold, because doubt has made us hesitant. We are too used to it crawling through our minds, like the serpent crawling through the tree in Eden, asking whether or not the experience is as compelling as it first seemed. We begin to have "second thoughts," which begin to qualify our enthusiasm for what we have experienced.

To the comment of the ancient sage Zeno — that some experiences are so powerful they force us to assent to their truth — we now wish to add the footnote, "I am not sure." Doubt is the parent of this uncertainty, and we feel obliged to practice it with a steady faithfulness because it is so intimately allied with our understanding of human nobility. We become one-sided in our vision, then, not seeing that the untempered passion that drives the prophet's life can be as much, or more, an expression of human nobility as the spirit of doubt.

It becomes difficult for us to appreciate the unqualified responsiveness of the prophets to their experience of God's call. (In all these comments on prophetic enthusiasm, however, see the comments in Chapter Six on prophetic reluctance, rather than doubt, even after the prophet becomes convinced of his or her calling as God's will.) We begin to hedge our bets against the legitimacy or intelligence of their enthusiasm. We become increasingly comfortable viewing them as eccentrics, or better, hysterics who have allowed their experiences to run away with them in an unreflective, unquestioning fashion. The unnerving awe we may have initially felt at their unreserved submission before God's call begins to metamorphose into condescension. No longer admiring their undoubting response to what they perceive is God's will, we now take this lack of doubt as cause for a more severe, less amiable judgment on them. Like their ancient critics, the accusation of willfulness starts growing in our minds. The thought emerges that their enthusiasm is basically an expression of pride, or in a more contemporary jargon, that they are on an "ego trip" that has blinded them to an objective appraisal of their behaviour. At an extreme we contend that they are guilty of blasphemy, the sacrilegious claim to know God's will simply to justify one's personal desires. Surely, the contempt many have had toward contemporary prophets like Dorothy Day and Daniel and Philip Berrigan is proof enough of this point.

The fundamental seduction of doubt is the feeling it creates that we are in control of what we are doing and where we are going. It is our consolation against all suspicions that we are mere automatons, slaves chanelled into patterns of behavior over which we have exercised no judgment. This doubting spirit is what prevents our full appreciation of the passivity with which the prophets greet their experience of God's call. We would prefer to sift this experience through our minds, calling it to account before the bar of our scepticism. Only as it survives this sifting, this accountability, are we willing to grant it a persuasiveness over our lives. The passivity of the prophets, therefore, their openness of mind to the experience of God's call, their complete receptivity to what has happened to them, is not for us. It seems slightly inhuman, animal-like. We are reminded of the passivity of the pet dog that is uncritically receptive to the calls of its master in shaping its behavior.

The danger in our attitude, however, though we rarely think of it, is that of an exaggerated self-esteem. It hasn't occurred to us that the passivity of the prophets before God's call, their receptivity when God speaks, indicates that conceit is not guiding their response to the experience. The testimony of Scripture is both eloquent and touching here. The passivity of the prophets is a consistent witness that they themselves have had no role in creating or controlling the experience that will henceforth guide their lives. It is a gift, and the only active agent involved in it is the Giver.

The experience of the call, in other words, is in no way self-structured; its influence is in no way dependent on the judgment of the prophet as to its legitimacy or effects. It occurs suddenly, unexpectedly, and without conscious motivation or determination on the prophet's part. This is one reason why the experience is so overwhelming: The prophet knows that its source lies completely outside himself or herself. The slightest suspicion that he or she had fashioned or contributed to it, that its legitimacy or persuasiveness were assisted by the activity of one's own mind — to that extent the experience would have been weakened in its influence. Were doubt ever to arise in the prophet's mind, in short, it would arise now. But it would be directed not at the experience itself but at the ways he or she may have distorted its effect through intruding, or better, interrupting an address whose source is God.

We can all think of countless examples of the way doubt can befuddle even the most powerful experiences we have. The college student who for years has been accumulating experiences indicating to her that she should devote her life to art, enters a studies program in business because her father has laid mortal doubts in her mind about her talent and success in pursuing art. This student has made a profound mistake in capitulating to her doubts, all the sadder because if left on her own, without the intrusion of her father, her enthusiasm for art would have been given a fair trial. Now it won't, and she will never know if it could have given her contentment in life, a sense of purpose and meaning that a business career never will. The student will come to know too late in life that some experiences are ignored or overruled only at the expense of personal integrity. You cannot be true to yourself and simultaneously deny your convictions. Certain that you are being called to direct your life one way, you ridicule yourself and make a mockery of your certainty, if you direct it any other.

What we are talking about is the phenomenon we otherwise call a vocation. The very word indicates its relationship to our remarks: "Vocation" derives from the Latin word *vocare*, meaning "to call." To have a vocation means to have the experience of being addressed in a persuasive way to shape your life in a certain fashion and not others. But maintaining a sense of vocation depends directly upon personal fidelity to the address, the call the individual has experienced. To the degree that doubt weaves its way into this fidelity, therefore, making it increasingly questionable, one's sense of vocation is weakened. From this weakening, of course, there might eventually come greater strength: We all know how doubt can be a crucible creating more intelligent, open-eyed commitments. But this cannot blind us to the fact that the weakening doubt brings can also continue until it kills a vocation. This is exactly what happened with the college student. The call to pursue her art that she felt so strongly, the untempered feeling that this pursuit should drive her life, became a whisper drowned out by the voice of doubt. Now it was only fleetingly heard — it would never become completely mute; a vocation never does — but it was no longer strong enough to command her life. But neither will it ever console her.

The sound it makes will never be a sedative for her mind, creating a wistful nostalgia for what might have been. The whisper will become a nagging, dripping thought that she cannot turn off. At one time she will be more conscious of it than at another; she may even have moments of complete forgetfulness, but the whisper cannot and will not leave her mind entirely, never to return. For it is embedded in her life like the pulse of her heart — part of her very being — and only death will finally silence it. Whenever a prophet tries to refuse the call of God, pretending that it does not exist or that its power is overestimated or merely passing, the prophet is caught in the same bind as the student and must be willing to accept the same consequences.

In a spiritual life gone haywire, where there are so many voices calling to us, each making demands requiring a response, consistency in life will be absent. Called in one direction and then another and then another, we will lose all sense of vocation. Our attentiveness scattered in a thousand different directions, answering a thousand different demands upon our time and talents, we become insufficiently attentive to the call that should dominate. We lose sight of the vocation that beckons us and gives a singular direction to all the paths our life may take.

In this situation our life begins to appear like a kaleidoscope; with every turn a different configuration of meaning and commitment confronts us with no apparent unity between them. It is a dizzying experience, a scattering of our consciousness all over the terrain of our life in a way that prohibits unity. We do not really know why we are doing what we do, only that we must do it. Nothing weaves our activity together except the bald fact that it is always we who are acting. There is nothing we can identify outside ourselves, some motive or purpose that embraces the deeds of our life and makes of them a whole, a plurality of activity held together by a common bond.

For the prophet this bond is the call of God. In every deed, in whatever activity, the unity of the prophet's behavior is provided by the certainty that God has called, and in calling requires a certain way to live. This is what creates both the passion that drives the prophet's life and the criterion for judging it. The prophet's God is a God who speaks. And the prophetic life is born from an experience of communication from God by means of which God's will is disclosed in a revelatory, that is, unambiguous way. Somehow — the fashions vary, though as we said they are all marked by passivity in the recipient — the prophet becomes aware that he or she has been addressed by God so compellingly that the experience cannot be ignored or diminished in importance.

Complete abandonment to it is required. The call, in brief, is the beginning of the prophet's vocation, and the vocation remains, as long as the call, continually remembered, exercises authority over behaviour. This, in fact, is the reason why memory plays so critical a role in prophetic spirituality. There is a constant recollection throughout the prophet's preaching to what God has done for his people, the way God has guided their lives individually and corporately. This recollection is a device for resurrecting, for making ever alive, the call of God as a persuasive influence in life. Should there be a slippage in this memory, then, or a blurring indifference toward it, the cohesion of the prophet's conviction that God is acting in his or her life, *just as God has acted in the lives of others,* would begin to weaken. Rather than seeing his or her own experience of God's call in continuity with the past experiences of others, the prophet would have to start seeing it as a freak, something without parallel in other human lives, and so indeed worthy of the most searching doubt as to its legitimacy. As we noted in the last chapter, this is one reason why the prophets refer so regularly to "the fathers." They intend to demonstrate by this reference that history has not been derelict of God's call to others, and that their own calls are thus not unique or new experiences in the story of the community. We might also note that the author of the epistle to the Hebrews seems to be getting at much the same idea in the famous prologue to his letter, "At various times and in different ways God has spoken in times past to the fathers . . . ." (Hebrews 1:1)

Now if we say that Christian living is prophetic in character, then it too must share this first trait of prophecy, the experience of being addressed by God. And so it does. Without exception the tradition of Christian spirituality speaks of the origin of the individual's desire to follow Jesus as a call from God (if when he speaks, for example, we assert that it is God himself speaking, then this call rings loudly and unambiguously in Jesus's own words, "Come, follow me!"). Or just as accurately said: Christian living is a vocation. It derives from an experience of being addressed by God in order to live out a message revealed by God, specifically now, the message of Jesus. It is this experience, in other words, that makes Christian living from its very beginning (and strictly speaking) a *theological* phenomenon, that is, an experience pertaining to the word and will of God.

But as with the call of the prophets, a vocation to Christian living will also endure as a vocation only as long as the initiating address by God, and the enthusiasm and conviction it creates regarding what God has revealed, is continually refreshed as an effective influence over the individual's life. Hearing God's call through passing days and years, like the refrain in a melody one cannot forget, the individual will be nourished and strengthened in the commitment that defines a Christian. Like the reminiscence of the beginning of their love, the experiences that brought it forth, that two people employ to help sustain their relationship, Christians must employ a similar reminiscence to help sustain their vocation.

In a culture like ours it is often difficult to maintain such enthusiasm. Almost everywhere we turn, from our advertising media to our governing economic and political theories, to our sophisticated concentration on the pre-eminent value of the individual, doubts arise as to the legitimacy of Christian living. The experience of being called to a Christian life, demonstrating in our own patterns of behavior fidelity to the words and deeds of Jesus, becomes increasingly inaudible among the noisiness of calls to cherish other values, to ignore as unrealistic the way of life taught by a noble but naive man. We thus lose our attentiveness to our vocation because no sooner have we turned our hearts and minds toward it than we are distracted by calls from other directions.

Yet, as we said earlier, the vocation never becomes entirely mute; its calling, now a whisper, can still be heard and only adds to our distraction. The call, "Follow me!" comes into conflict with invitations to follow other ways of living, so that our mind is set against itself because doubt has been born in our certainty about following Jesus. Our vocation as Christians consequently becomes an open question, and we realize that if the words of God are written on our hearts, as Jeremiah contends (31:31), and not on tablets of stone, it is not only God who is writing there. Other words from other sources are written there as well, drawing our attention, dividing our hearts, and leaving us confused and weary.

In this situation we must find some way to resurrect our enthusiasm for Christian living. We must recollect in a vivid way the witness of Jesus, and through this recollection allow the witness to become increasingly a formative element in how we think and feel. This, of course, has always been the encouragement of Christian spirituality in the face of doubt or a wearying confusion about the meaning and demands of Christian living.

It is expressed pre-eminently through an emphasis on the *liturgical* character ingredient in any attempt to follow Jesus. As the reader knows, all liturgy has three fundamental aspects, each associated with a particular temporal phase of human existence. There is the aspect of the past (in a technical theological vocabulary, the *anamnetic* character of liturgy), the aspect of the future (again in technical vocabulary, the *propleptic* character of liturgy), and of course the aspect of the present. Of these three aspects, the past or anamnetic has priority since it is on the basis of our recollection of past events (the words and deeds, the destiny of Jesus) that we shape our future hope, and on the basis of our memory and hope that we shape the criteria for our present behavior.

Without an enthusiasm for the past, its continual refreshment in our minds and hearts, the future would be blind and the present sterile. Whenever you have participated in a Christian liturgy, therefore, and this refreshment has not occurred (just as would be the case if your hope had not been tapped or your present behaviour challenged) the liturgy has been a failure. By extension, we may offer the same judgment on the exercise of any Christian prayer, private or communal. Whenever you pray and your memory of Jesus has not been revivified, your prayer has gone awry. For it has failed to alert you again to the call that animates all Christian living, the vocation that lures you through life despite all your doubts and hesitancy, the call of discipleship. Whenever the present becomes kaleidescopic in the directions it is pulling you, whenever the future appears as simply a continuation of this kaleidoscopic indirection, you must remember the past. Resurrect the witness of your Lord and permit his living voice to guide you. This is the first trait, the first counsel of all Christian prophecy.

A REMINISCENCE

Let me conclude this chapter with a personal reminiscence. It complements the point just made and also explains why I proceeded as I did throughout these remarks on the vocation of the Christian prophet. When I was a young boy my mother told me a little story about God. But instead of saying, as I had frequently heard, that a part of us resides in God, she took just the opposite tack. She said that before we are born God puts a part of *himself* — but only a part — within us, and that throughout our lives this part is always searching to find the rest of God so that it can be happy. She called this part of God in each of us our soul, and said that its searching for the rest of God was called faith. And only when the soul has completed its task, having finally found God and become whole, can we be happy.

Even at the time, however, I had difficulty with the idea behind her little story, for I remember how much it reminded me of the game "hide and seek." Rather, I thought that if God exists, then surely he must be everywhere all at once, and not divided into parts. And if God is everywhere, then why do I have to spend my life looking for him? All of God ought to be right next to me, even within me, so that to see and find him I should only have to open my eyes.

As I grew older I held to this opinion, except for the discovery that seeing correctly involved more than just opening my eyes. It also involved focusing them correctly. In other words, if I wanted to see God I would not only have to open my eyes, which at times was hard enough to do, but I would also have to adjust them to my surroundings. Otherwise I would not be able to see clearly, and would perhaps mistake a blurred vision of God for a true one. With this one slight alteration, then, I came to agree with my mother: Life was indeed a search for God, but this search was not so much an attempt to find God, as if he were hiding, as it was to see him clearly in ourselves and the world around us.

At some point in their lives many people probably think seriously of devoting themselves to this search for a clear vision of God. But as other interests begin to intrude, they become convinced that this is only the fervor of an idealistic mind, and that a realistic view of life, with all its cares, requires its dismissal. Concern for material security, for example, might gradually become a primary demand on their time and efforts, which they cannot ignore, so that from their one-time thought that seeing God correctly was to be preferred to all the goods of the world, they have come to think that worldly goods are the only good. To pursue a vision of God, then, becomes but a dreamlike fantasy that would only distract them from the real goal of their lives, or worse, pose a dangerous threat to it.

Yet, despite their judgment on the danger or distraction of pursuing a vision of God, God is not so easily forgotten. There is still that part of God within them my mother had spoken of, and it marks them like a wound whose pain periodically returns, like the wound Isaiah must have suffered when his lips were touched with burning coals. And the truth it reminds them of is this: When the wound is allowed to heal, and its pain no longer comes, they have lost not only their souls but also their God.

Jesus speaks of those who have eyes to see, but do not see (Mark 8:18), referring to the peculiar stubborness of the human mind whenever it willfully refuses to judge or appreciate accurately even the most compelling experiences or commonplace truths. The Pharisees are the principal target of his comment, though to varying degrees it applies to each of us. For whatever reason — pride, fear, indifference — we blur and distort our vision so that seeing clearly becomes difficult if not impossible for us. The clear-headedness that is partnered with clear-sightedness gives way to lack of conviction in how we think, an uncertainty regarding the truth of our experiences that we often overcome by a simple act of blind assertion.

What I am talking about here we may otherwise describe as one effect of the phenomenon of *bias*. The word "bias" means slant or angle and originates as a description of certain techniques in weaving and agriculture. When used as a metaphor describing our ways of thinking or feeling, it implies that we are approaching a given experience indirectly, from a certain angle that automatically provides a context for the way we will understand the experience.

You can experience the prophetic witness of Jesus contained in the New Testament from a variety of angles, each reflecting a personal bias you may have. This is what gives it its relevance, its amazing adaptability to individual lives. But in the process great care must also be exercised that one's angle of vision is not also a distortion of the witness, a convenience that has elimated less appealing elements of the witness. For then the individual can too easily fall prey to practicing self-concern (one sees what one wants to see) rather than self-abandonment (one sees what is there). Anyone can readily succumb to the blindness that does not see what Jesus teaches in myriad ways, but perhaps nowhere more clearly than in the simple injunction, "Only the one who loses his life will save it" (Luke 17:33).

The task my mother said would be mine — finding God in my life — is thus the task of every Christian. But to find where God is present in life must be embraced wholeheartedly, in a committed self-abandonment that knows no qualifications, no limits. Or like anyone who practices a passionate faith, every Christian must embrace a vocation, the call of God that beckons us sometimes gently, sometimes forcefully through life.

QUESTIONS FOR REFLECTION AND DISCUSSION

1. What happens to the meaning of life when you believe you have been called by God to live a certain way (say, as an artist or physician, or religiously, a Christian), and then you ignore this call?

2. If asked, what criteria would you use to determine that a given claim on your life represents God's will?

3. Should the wise individual pass all statements and proposals regarding how to live through a process of personal doubt, and, if needed, even seek the doubts of others in this process? Explain.

4. What might a contemporary psychological assessment be of the prophetic enthusiasm described in this chapter?

5. We spoke about the call of the prophet as the experience establishing his or her vocation. What would you consider three essential ingredients in the vocation of being a Christian in the world today — ingredients, that is, the absence of any one of which would cease making a person a Christian?

QUESTIONS FOR REFLECTION AND DISCUSSION

CHAPTER THREE

The Authority

T he second trait of prophetic life is easy enough to describe, since it follows logically from the first. Because the prophets assert that their call, their vocation, finds its source in God, and because the experience of being called convinces them of the rightness of some revelation of God's will, they possess an authority they otherwise would not. Specifically, the authority is to preach the revelation, to manifest by word and deed the conviction that God's word is known. Thus Jeremiah (26:15) voices a sentiment found continually among the Old Testament prophets:

> Do whatever you please or think right with me. But be sure of this, that if you put me to death you will be bringing innocent blood on yourselves, on this city and on its citizens, *since Yahweh has truly sent me to you to say all these things in your hearing.*

The call of the prophets, then, is not a dead-end experience. It is not simply an aesthetic event, like listening to a piece of fine music, that need not go beyond itself to establish its meaning or purpose. Rather, the call brings in its train certain results; and the degree to

37

which the call is effective over the prophet's life, the meaning or purpose it will hold, is proportionate to the degree to which the results are effective. One of these is the authority the prophet possesses; three others will be taken up in each of the following three chapters.

Theologically speaking, the only *unquestionable* authority human beings can hold over each other is one derived from God. Left on their own, in other words, there is an equity among humans that can be rescinded only by force or deception. By this I mean that any authority that does not have its source outside the circle of humanity — any claim by some human beings to determine the lives and destinies of other human beings — is an authority we are either forced or cheated into recognizing. The prophets are extraordinarily sensitive to this point, of course, and so practice an amazing diligence in reminding their listeners that the authority they exercise is not self-generated but something given them by God. We have already noted the way they describe the experience of their call in relation to this point. The authority of the prophet, like the experience of the call preceding it, is something the prophet has only received. It is a donation, freely bestowed and unearned, not something belonging to the prophet by right.

We will see in Chapter Six that the prophet's attitude toward this authority, far from being greeted with expectation, is greeted with considerable reluctance. For there is a continual temptation to view the experience of being called by God in much the same way that some mystics in Christian tradition have viewed their own ecstatic experiences. That is to say, there is a temptation to release the experience from its implied responsibilities and make it an end in itself, something to be privately enjoyed and described to others but not serving as a catalyst for future activity. In this situation the prophet has become stuck in what the Greeks called *theoria*, without moving into the realm of *praxis*, the concrete and relevant application of their experience to the world around them. It is this same failure, for example, that was also one of the fundamental criticisms of Marx against Hegel, that Hegel did not provide an adequate analysis of specific patterns of behavior that would enflesh his philosophical ideas, as well as being the source of Gabriel Marcel's lifelong battle against what he called "the spirit of abstraction."

Let us take a closer look, then, at this authority of the prophet. We will first look at forms of authority that have their source within the circle of humanity, that is, an experience of God's revealed will. These forms derive either from force or deception.

BREAKING THE CIRCLE OF HUMANITY: ON FORCE, DECEPTION, AND REVELATION

Authority from force is the typical form in which authority is both exercised and experienced. Its essential ingredient is the notion of *office* or position, and it presumes a hierarchical structure in human community. Specifically, it depends on the community's acceptance that some of its members possess the capacity or power (legitimately or not) to determine the behavioral patterns of all the members. The parenthetical qualification is important. When authority exercises its power illegitimately we speak of a tyranny; when the exercise is legitimate we speak of a democracy. The basis of this judgment is that we are dealing here with an authority that derives its rights only from within the circle of humanity. As such, it must reflect the will of all (or at least the majority of) members within the circle if it is to function legitimately. Otherwise, when reflecting only the will of some (or minority of) members, it is truncated and therefore unrepresentative.

To be sure, in both cases the members of the community are still subject to the will of those in authority. But in the first case their submission is the result of their participation in the community's life, specifically in the decisions regarding who will structure and enforce the behavioral expectations of the community. In the second case, however, their submission is the result of a simple rise to dominance (through whatever means) of those in authority and their ensuing power to exercise their will without accountability over the other members of the community. In the first case, behavioral expectations are communally determined, however indirectly; in the second case, they are not. This description, I trust, while simply stated, is not simple-minded but lucid and sufficient in suggesting valid distinctions in the complex phenomenon of human communal organization. We will be returning to it in a variety of ways in the following pages.

One of the enduring topics of human conversation centers on the respective merits of these methods for establishing authority within human communities (though my own preference should be obvious from the descriptions I gave each). Even a study of so venerable an institution as the ancient Greek city-state leaves us in distressing ambiguity regarding a clear choice between them. In the Athenian democracy at the time of Plato, for example, many political theorists argued for free participation by all (free adult males) in establishing and limiting the authority of those charged with government. Yet, in his treatises *The Republic, The Statesman,* and *The Laws,* Plato himself argues that the inadvertence and irrationality of most human beings when they make decisions suggest that only an "enlightened" few should possess and exercise authority over the community — and before the inadvertence and irrationality of the other members (in an embarrassing comment he isolates poets for special criticism) practice a severe and uncompromising discipline.

What these two viewpoints represent is a clash between confidence in the prevailing good will and intelligence of human beings, and scepticism toward this goodness and intelligence born of an overload of data regarding the human capacity for stupidity and a self-serving contempt of others. In a contemporary and somewhat condescending parlance we would say that they represent a clash between idealism (the Athenian theorists) and realism (Plato) regarding human nature. I say this because most of us, in an alarming though rarely examined bias, tend to define realism by the degree to which individuals acknowledge and defend themselves against the depravity that courses through human existence. It is the only "sensible" attitude, we think, that can result whenever we have been ricocheted off the malice and wickedness of other human beings. At an extreme it leads us to support the idea that authority in a community has as its primary task the deterrence of human vice rather than the promotion of human virtue. Or differently said: We become insensitive to the idea that any true realism must reflect a balanced appreciation of both the good and evil human beings are capable of and the clear intent to structure authority in a community so as to enhance the good.

The authority we referred to above is governmental or political in nature. We are talking about those members of a community who occupy offices or positions (president, parent, judge, etc.) that give them the right to initiate and/or enforce laws determining the behavioral patterns of the community. The authority here exercised, in other words, is extrinsic to what your own convictions might be regarding proper modes of human conduct, so that whether or not your convictions prevail as the standard of conduct, you still submit to the current laws. Or, if you cannot do so with integrity, you willingly embrace the consequences when they are enforced. The point is that the authority that counsels your behavior in this situation always emerges from within the circle of humanity. Its source is not a revelation of God's will but an assessment of what is needed because human beings have gathered together in a community. We will not belabor the common-sense insight that whenever they congregate for the well-being of all, human beings must organize themselves into some form of hierarchical structure, although we will again take up this particular form of authority when discussing the political involvement of the prophet in Chapter Five.

There is another form of authority, however, that can also exercise force over us. It is more personally engaged than the form described above, and the continuation of its character as an authority is directly dependent on our permitting it to remain so. I am speaking about what the Greeks called the *kalos kalgathos*, the authority of the wise individual, who then becomes our teacher. We have discovered in someone a persuasiveness of vision, an adeptness in analyzing the meaning of events, a sensitivity that cuts through to the truth of our experiences, and we submit ourselves to him or her. The authority here is not basically political in nature (though it may become that, if the teacher gathers sufficient disciples, as Gandhi in India) but moral. It is the power of personal example, the integrity and clear-headedness we find in what the teacher says and does that is the catalyst luring us to place our lives under his or her will.

When we fail in this submission we acknowledge the force being exercised over us in the form of guilt: We have betrayed the teacher, and thus ourselves, by betraying our conviction that the teacher should be followed without reserve. Correspondingly, when we succeed in this submission, we acknowledge the force being exercised over us in the form of contentment: We have been true to the teacher, and thus ourselves, by remaining faithful to our conviction that the teacher should always be followed. In either case, the teacher is clearly someone with whom we have aligned our judgments of self-worth, and our failure or fidelity before the guidance he or she provides is fundamentally self-directed. Following the teacher has become the criterion for judging whether or not we have been true to ourselves.

The danger in all discipleship, of course, just as it is the danger in political forms of authority, is slavery. By submitting to the rule of someone else, the individual may too readily abdicate personal responsibility over life that is rightfully his or hers (and no one else's). Discipleship and hierarchical government both have built into them the temptation to prefer security over freedom, being told what to do rather than having to decide it for oneself. Any boy (or girl) who refuses to achieve a sense of personal independence would be an excellent case in point. He has existed for years under both the governmental and moral authority of his parents. And while he has at times found this irritating, his overall attitude is one of satisfaction with this situation. For it absolves him from accountability for his life. For all the mistakes he makes, the indiscretions and foolishness in his decisions, he has a handy scapegoat in parental authority: "I only did what you told me." "Why did you let me do that?" "You should have stopped me." The litany goes through all its various expressions but really meaning only one thing: The boy prefers that others assume responsibility for his life because of a fear to exercise personal freedom, the need to make choices.

Those familiar with his great work, *The Brothers Karamazov*, will recognize that we are living here in the world of Dostoevski's Grand Inquisitor. The Inquisitor is anyone who justifies the authority he or she possesses over others on the premise that this is exactly what they want. The Inquisitor is always willing to play the wise, decisive, judicious parent for any individual who refuses to develop his or her own wisdom, decisiveness, and judgment.

There is a distressing inhumanity in the above individual's viewpoint; all the more so if it has been willingly nourished. Yet, it would be naive not to recognize that it may also have been nourished *for* the individual. We all know parents, for example, who have intentionally sustained their child's dependence on them beyond the age when this dependence can be legitimately defended. Although they would never admit it, this manoeuver is fundamentally an act of conceit on their part. They have found an appealing contentment in the god-like role they played in their child's early years, have attached their own sense of personal value to it, and are reluctant to give it up. No god or goddess easily steps down from a pedestal.

The same observation can apply in the broader arena of political authority. The seduction that has created every tyrant who has ever walked the earth is that the people governed are still children who need such tyranny; they do not have the capacity to exercise an intelligent responsibility for their lives. The tyrant, however, continues to walk the earth only because the people agree (or do not disagree seriously enough) with his or her assessment of them. They have yet to experience the untempered feeling of communion, telling them that within the closed circle of humanity all are equal, and that the authority enjoyed by some is enjoyed only by the will of the others. Tyranny can be sustained only as long as the tyrant is successful in isolating and fragmenting the members of a community from each other. Suspicion is the key to every tyrant's success, the ability to create and maintain within the members a gnawing doubt regarding anyone else's talent to organize and guide the community in a humane and harmonious way toward some valued goal.

When a child has been reared in a healthy fashion, as occurs similarly in the case of a healthy society, the assumption by others of an authority they do not rightly possess will inevitably elicit rebellion. Every worthy parent knows this at those points in a child's development when petulant or contradictory behavior is in effect telling the parent, "I wish to begin taking responsibility for my life." It is a hard and trying experience for the parent, especially in those instances when the child's decisions are clearly wrong-headed and will bring pain and frustration. The overwhelming instinct of the parent is to intervene and spare the child the coming grief. But the worthy parent does not, knowing not only that the child will rebel against this intervention but that the child's mistakes are often the most effective training ground for the development of a more mature, intelligent, and informed responsibility over life.

The same applies in society at large to those who exercise a worthy authority there. They too will realize that behavior of the members of the society (or large numbers of them) that begins to consistently contradict their guidance is a clear indication that this guidance is intruding on the members' sense of personal responsibility, their pre-eminent right to decide how they will live, including how they will live with each other. The worthy leader will here abdicate or adjust the exercise of authority so that this responsibility, this right is given clear recognition and approval — even, like the worthy parent, when the leader thinks it will lure the members into mistaken, possibly pain-producing decisions.

The second of the two sources of authority we said exists within the circle of humanity — authority gained and/or exercised by deception — is easy enough to understand. It is simply an unpleasant wrinkle on authority gained and exercised by force. For now it is through deceit, lies, and misdirections, that those in authority exercise their power. The deception works because it creates either extraordinary fear or extraordinary hope in the members of the society. A president of the United States, for example, who wishes to build up a military arsenal lies about the aggressive power of a potential enemy, their malice and unqualified will to dominate others. The fear created through this deception causes the members of the society to assign him whatever authority he needs to increase weaponry. Or he promises them an old age in which they will have sufficient funds to care for their needs, and the hope he creates through this deception causes them to assign him an authority to exact exorbitant, demeaning taxes.

This is the same sort of deception we find in the smaller society of the family whenever a parent creates unrealistic fears or hopes in a child only to maintain authority over him or her. If the deceit is practiced enough, well maintained and cultured, it can safeguard the authority of the parent (or in the former case, the politician) with an amazing tenacity.

If and when the deception is unveiled, however, the expected result can only be rebellion. For no society, not even a family, can be asked to harbor a liar in authority. To do so would be the same as asking it to dissolve whatever order and sense of common purpose it possesses into a chaos of unreliability and mistrust. A dizzying process of increasing brutality, disrespect for others, and defensive self-concern would then ensue, which can only end in the society's quick and depressing extinction.

It is only when the circle of humanity is broken, when the will of God intervenes in the history of human development, that human authority deriving from force or deception becomes a meaningless issue. This, of course, is exactly the experience of the prophets. The authority with which they speak is one to which they have been elected, to be sure; but the election takes place not as the result of human concourse but by the free agency of God. The result of this experience, inerrantly affirmed by the prophets, is that their authority can thus be relieved not by any human being or group of human beings but only by God. The clarity of their position is indicated in a variety of ways, but perhaps nowhere more forcefully than in the typical refrain employed to reiterate before others the will of God revealed to them: "Thus says the Lord . . . ."

With this statement the prophet is clearly separating whatever authority he or she may possess as an individual from the authority of the words about to be spoken. In the prophets' minds, as against what frequently happens in our own, there is no confusion between personal opinions and the received will of God. Admittedly, this might initially impress us as being uncomfortably close to demagoguery, the manipulative arrogance that causes an individual to use any means, including the claim to know God's will, to secure power over others. But before this initial impression starts brooding in our minds we must cut it short (if we are to be fair to the prophet) by recalling again the nature of the prophetic call described in the last chapter, particularly the prophet's passivity while experiencing it. Further reasons for doing so will occupy us in Chapter 6 when discussing the prophet's reluctance.

For the prophet there can be no decisive meaning attached to human authority when the authority of the will of God is available. Moreover, there is no one who can contravene this authority except God himself. As we will see in Chapter Five, it is precisely this perception that regularly places the Old Testament prophets in conflict with the kings of Israel and Judah. When God's will is known, the prophet will say, there can be only one legitimate response before its authority, submission.

There can be no legitimate rebellion here, in other words, as there can be against authority that is humanly generated. For what standard could prevail to justify this rebellion that would have preeminence over the will of God? The answer is as clear to the prophets as the noonday sun: none. The preached will of God has final authority; it is compelling and must be encouraged with intelligence and passion, for no other reason than that it is the will of God. Unlike all authority humanly generated whenever people gather in a community with mutual values and goals, the authority of God is alone self-justifying. And to this the propeht will add, absolute. The prophet can present no reasoned or logical argument for this viewpoint, however, except as it might derive from the faith that there is a God, that this God is interested in the course of human development, and that this interest is expressed in the revelation of his will. In the prophetic view, reason and logic emerge only subsequently to the act of faith. They can sustain faith, strengthening its persuasiveness, intelligibility, and application in everyday life, but they cannot create or ground it.

Equal to the prophets' insistence on the absolute force of God's will, its unqualified authority, is their insistence upon the truth of this will. There can be no deception in the activity of God, no false fears or hopes employed to gain or embellish the prophets' authority. The authority resides not only in the fact that it is God who has spoken but in the fact that God's speech is simultaneously joined to the truth. And so with the refrain that establishes the authority of what the prophet speaks ("Thus says the Lord . . .") we find as the familiar partner the refrain, "You have heard the words of the Lord and his words are true." The idea of a deceitful God, a God who manipulates the fears or hopes of human beings without truthful intent, would have drawn from the prophets an untempered feeling of disgust. Then, indeed, rebellion against God would have become a possibility, even more, a responsibility.

In fact, rebellion such as this is what the prophets continuallly encourage against "idols," "false gods" that create false fears and hopes in human hearts. The polemic of Elijah against the claims Jezabel makes for her deities is an eloquent example of this. Jonah's contempt for the gods of Ninevah is another. Jesus' refusal of the God taught by the Parisees is a third. In all cases, what the prophet is pointing out is the calamity that would result if, in addition to relating to lying human beings, we also had to relate to a lying God. Then every authority that would guide our lives — all authority within and without the circle of humanity — would be forever prey to our scepticism, the recurring suspicion that the authority is unreliable, deceiving and misguiding our lives. What would remain to us then would be an utter relativism in which values and goals were determined by each individual alone without benefit of further appraisal. The world would become a madhouse of egomaniacs.

ABSOLUTE AND RELATIVE AUTHORITY

We can capture the second trait of the prophetic life differently by speaking of the *extraordinariness* of the witness it requires. For if an individual is indeed convinced that he or she has been addressed by God to preach God's revelation of his will — for Christians, contained pre-eminently in the words and deeds of Jesus — then this individual's preaching, what he or she does and says, this person's whole life will become suffused with the authority this conviction provides. This individual will now preach and live with a certainty that was absent before the conviction. But again, as with the call preceding it, we must note that this authority is something he or she is only the passive recipient of. The authority, in other words, is something given by another, not something that belongs to the individual by right.

In other books I have stressed that this conviction is born of the practice of obedience, and I have noted that this is not first defined as the submission of our will to the will of another, but by the quality of attentiveness we bring to an object under our consideration. I draw this understanding from the meaning of the word itself. "Obedience" derives from the Latin prefix ob-plus the word *audire*. The prefix functions as an intensive and *audire* means "to hear" or "to listen." Obedience (*ob* + *audire*) thus means to hear or listen intently, thoroughly, without distraction. It is the type of concentrated devotion that presumably characterizes our prayer, study, and reflection. It is definitely the type of concentrated devotion that characterizes the response of the prophets when they hear (*audire*) the call of God. It is what allows any of us, in other words, to shape the convictions that guide our life: Through our devotion to what we have heard we become convinced of its truth or falsity.

This is what St. Paul is also getting at in his famous dictum, "Faith (conviction) comes through hearing" (Romans 10:17). The hearing he has in mind is what we have just described as obedience. But since the apostle, like all the prophets before him, presumes that the words of God are by nature true, the purpose of obedience cannot be to establish the legitimacy of what God has said; rather, its purpose is to establish the individual's fidelity to God's word as an active and persuasive influence in life. To be obedient, in short, is fundamentally always an act of personal loyalty (to one's convictions), just as to be disobedient is fundamentally always an act of personal disloyalty, or in more traditional terms, a sin against oneself.

Whenever Christians lose sight of this fact, whenever they begin to think it is they themselves who are the source of the authority with which they preach their conviction regarding the message of Jesus — by their education, for example, or their intuitive abilities, or more crassly, their "winning personalities" — they have slipped into the arrogance, the self-righteousness to which Jesus devoted his most telling criticisms. Instead of issuing in humility and gratitude, the authority that derives from the experience of their call issues in conceit. They have forgotten that the words they give their obedience to are not their own words but the words of God, that the ultimate source of their convictions thus resides not within but outside themselves. They become what the Old Testament consistently condemns as "false prophets," individuals who have lost sight of the origin of the authority with which they preach.

Or differently: What the false prophets do is to re-confine their authority within the circle of humanity, in this case their own humanity. As such, however, their authority becomes relative, no longer expressing the divine will but only a human will among countless other human wills. And the final criterion for judging this authority consequently becomes its utility or effectiveness in changing circumstances rather than its inherent potential for universal application.

The ultimate concern of all false prophets, in other words, is to guarantee the success of their authority in direct proportion to its expediency in *this* given situation. The ultimate concern of all true prophets, on the other hand, does not involve the question of success, and certainly not the expediency with which their authority is practiced, but only the fidelity it manifests toward the will of God. That is why so many of the true prophets were tortured and ridiculed, while false prophets have had an amazing history of personal advantage and good fortune. As we will see in the following pages, though, this is not the same as saying that the true prophet is indifferent to the issue of the relevant application of God's will to changing circumstances. The true prophet is concerned, very emphatically.

For the true prophet, then, authority is absolute only when it comes from God; otherwise it is relative. By this I mean that the word of God, from the prophetic viewpoint, is not capable of abrogation but only interpretation by those receiving it. When Yahweh speaks his condemnations against idol worship in the Old Testament, for example, he does not offer any qualifications. He does not say, "Do not worship any graven images *except* . . . ." There is no exception to the command he speaks, and no exception can thus be structured into the command by those hearing it. What the hearers are left with, rather, is the task of interpreting the command. Does it mean, for example, that they cannot eat food, good food, that has been consecrated in rituals of idol worship? Is doing so breaking the intent of the command, its control over human behavior? Or again, does the command extend beyond its hearers? Must its hearers attempt to stamp out the idol worship of their neighbors? Or may this worship be tolerated until they too become hearers of the word of Yahweh in a way that opens their minds to the rightness of the command? The command stands; it is absolute and unabridgeable. But frequently its meaning and application is left to the interpretive insight of its hearers.

This clearly places an uneasy task on them, however, and the liberation it requires — the freedom to live out one's convictions about God's will in a faithful way — is only initially seductive. After a while, with a full life of this freedom facing them head on, day in and day out, it becomes onerous, a burden they may wish to abdicate. Then, as we said earlier, they become subject to the attraction of an Inquisitor, a master under whom discipleship is a euphemism for slavery. No longer wanting the authority to make their own decisions about how to live, they hand it over to someone else.

Christians, of course, often find themselves in a situation similar to the one above regarding the specific commands of Jesus. When Jesus mandates the behavioral pattern, "Be generous," for example, he offers no qualifications. Like Yahweh in the Old Testament, he does not say, "Be generous *except* . . . ." No, the command is absolute, and any abridgement of it is something forced upon it by its hearers.

But how is the command to be interpreted? What does the hearer who recognizes its unlimited authority do to meet the command? How is the hearer to apply it in his or her own life? Toward these questions the hearer must exercise the same interpretive insight we mentioned above. After all, the way the command might have been interpreted in the Jerusalem of Jesus' day, when beggars could have regularly appeared at the door, would have to be considerably different for those followers of Jesus who live in an American suburb, where beggars appear only in the literature they read.

In all instances the Christian must submit to the authority of the command, and to those who continually rehearse it in their preaching, but *how* each one does so is left to the formative insight of his or her own conscience. Or to make the same point differently: The trust that Jesus manifests in his life applies not only to his trust in his Father but to his trust in his disciples as well. Jesus teaches in a fashion that makes clear his confidence that his disciples will take his words seriously, seek to understand them, and faithfully attempt to apply them in their lives, even when he knows this task will at times be difficult. He demonstrates nothing of the suspicion that infiltrates some teachers and causes them to qualify their teaching in a thousand different ways that, in effect, allows it to be understood or applied in only one way. For Jesus, in short, imagination is a respected element in human consciousness.

We may conclude, then, that although there is an absoluteness in the authority of the revealed will of God in both Testaments, there is a remarkable relativity in the way this will can be applied in the specific circumstances of day-to-day living. Jesus is especially clear on this point, and repeatedly refuses any attempt to give an absolute quality to our applications of God's spoken will that only the authority of God's word can command. This, in fact, becomes one of the major points of controversy in his relationship with the Pharisees. He is uncomfortable with their willingness to give their understanding of God's will a sanctity that no human understanding can possess. And he is unremitting in his condemnation of the arrogance with which they frequently preached this understanding. The type of Phariseeism that Jesus criticizes, therefore, must meet a similar criticism at the hands of his disciples whenever it re-emerges (as it often has) in the course of their own history. Only the words of God are in themselves holy; human words are holy only to the degree that they mirror the words of God.

COMPANIONSHIP WITH OTHERS:
ON POWER AND PERSUASION

Political authority is one that legislates; prophetic authority is one that persuades. In the first case, authority is a laying down of laws; in the second case, it is an appeal to a way of life. Political authority is premissed on a *quid pro quo* relationship between two contracting parties (those who govern, those who are governed) in which abiding by the law issues in reward, and breaking the law issues in punishment. Prophetic authority is premissed on an appreciation of single-mindedness, the "purity of heart" Jesus spoke of, in which the good is done for no other reason than that it is good. Prophetic authority does not raise the question of rewards and punishments, or at least it does so only secondarily to its main concern that the good be done for its own sake.

Political authority has its source within the closed circle of humanity; it is parental, civil, ecclesiastical, and so on. Only as it becomes prophetic does it break this circle and become theological as well, God-directed in character. The only will that can be understood as good in itself is the will of God. And the task of prophetic authority is to persuade others, first, that this is so, and then that God's will is known. The prophet in any age exists as a living reminder that we have not been orphaned in a hostile world where human whim reigns as the final arbiter of what becomes of us. The prophet coaxes from our minds a continual recollection of the presence of God in the story of human development.

Like political authority, however, prophetic authority can go awry in its intentions. When it does, it becomes especially demonic in its expressions because it backs itself up with the very authority of God, and the claim that its rights and power are therefore unquestionable. This is the stance of all religious maniacs who do not perceive that their reception of a revelation of God's will does not bring in its train an identification between their own will and God's, or that their interpretations of God's will do not possess the sanctity of the will itself. They have obliterated the chasm that separates the words of God from their own words, and thus have lifted the barrier between the object of their faith and their specific attempts to articulate it.

Religious maniacs do not understand that they can legitimately mediate the authority possessed by God's word, but that this mediation cannot generate any claim to an authority apart from God's word. They are behaviorally deviant because their imagination has gone wild on the thought that their ways are identical to God's ways in the world. They demand an unquestioning and complete submission to the instruction contained in what they say and do. And when they don't get it, when they see in the response of others even potential disagreement or contradiction, they tend to become belligerent and threatening. Sometimes they can back up their threats personally; they have the authority (of whatever sort) to punish those who disagree with them. But in all cases they threaten the punishment of God, the divine retribution that will inevitably recompense eye for eye and tooth for tooth any rebellion against what they proclaim is the word of God. Prophetic humility, the awareness that one can preach only what has been received from God — that one cannot go beyond this when voicing promises of reward and punishment — is completely foreign to them.

The demon in Milton's great poem, *Paradise Lost,* thus becomes a classic illustration of all religious maniacs. His screaming confession, "Better to reign in hell than serve in heaven," is the manifesto *in extremis* of anyone who refuses or has forgotten the distinction (what Kierkegaard calls "the infinite qualitative difference") between one's own will and God's will. All religious maniacs commit the elemental fault the Greeks called *hubris,* the assertion that they, finally, are the arbiters of values, the judges of life and death, the minds that will determine the course of creation, because they, finally, are the ones to whom the will of God is accessible.

We are in the world of the psychopathic prophet who determined the destiny of Germany for a dozen years, and the one in Jonestown who manipulated the communal suicide of a small population. The madhouse scenarios of prophets gone awry in their authority are familiar to us all. They are written in grotesque detail on countless pages of history. And they remind us that human savagery is never quite so exquisite as when it is attached to a religious conviction gone haywire. The greatest villains who have ever brought ruin into human communities have been those convinced that their activity has the blessing of God; that they are serving a providential scheme, the "order of things," against which any rebellion deserves a hellish reply. The villainy is born from an untempered conceit leading them to think that because they have received a revelation of God's will, they may begin to act like God, enjoying divine prerogatives in determining the values and goals, life and death of other human beings.

Whenever a society is caught with a dearth of leaders, whenever its members are looking for someone who will exercise an authority that will guide meaning into their lives, the society is open to the influence of a prophet. But the true prophet, unlike the false or insane one, will exercise this authority only as a parenthesis, a hiatus in the development of the society. By this I mean that whereas false or insane prophets have invested their own worth in the authority they exercise, and hence will maneuver events to maintain and strengthen this authority, the tack of true prophets is just the opposite. Their authority is exercised only as long as it is needed, that is, until the time when the people they preach to have themselves become prophets, exercising their own authority over their lives.

True prophets, in other words, seek to bring people to an experience of God similar to their own, so that from this experience a vocation will be shaped that will give the people the leadership they yearn for. Once this task is complete, their authority, no longer needed or productive, is gladly abdicated. False or insane prophets, on the other hand, would die before they did likewise.

What engages true prophets is fundamentally the task of catechesis. Their purpose is to instruct people that the will of God is known and must be taken seriously, but that it cannot be taken seriously until these same people assign it authority over their lives. Unlike false prophets, however, they view themselves in this task only as mediators, not initiators, of what God wills, and so are able to withdraw from it with satisfied hearts when it is complete.

True prophets know that what they preach does not have value in and of itself simply because it is they who are preaching it; rather, it has value because (and only when) it mirrors the received word of God. True prophets, in short, readily acknowledge the distinction between what the Greeks called *doxa* (personal opinion) and *episteme* (true knowledge); the former comes from the workings of their own minds, the latter from the revealed word of God. But false prophets not only blur this distinction, they do away with it entirely, equating their personal opinions with true knowledge.

As we said earlier, at a certain stage of development every healthy child achieves a maturity of consciousness that increasingly allows him or her to make decisions apart from parental leadership, which can be an extraordinarily disconcerting experience for the parents. To benefit from it they must come to the realization that their child is becoming more and more like them, that is, a thinking, valuing creature who is providing a meaning for life whose source is a "calling" or vocation that must be pursued. If the parents do not come to this realization, if they attempt to deafen the child to the calling or vocation being experienced, they are in effect assaulting the very beginnings of the child's sense of integrity. Their behavior now becomes analagous to that of the false or insane prophet. It amounts to a refusal to abdicate an authority over the child's life that no longer belongs to them, but now belongs to the child. And if the child is not strong, if the vocation dies under the parental refusal to relinquish authority over him or her, then the child becomes much more accurately described not as their partner in life, someone with whom they share an equal communion, but as their slave.

The textbooks of psychoanalysis are filled with case histories describing just this type of situation. The adult who cannot make critical decisions without the consultation and approval of a parent or parent-surrogate will be psychologically stymied when this parental authority is no longer available. The initial impulse then will be to transfer as quickly as possible onto someone else, a new "parent," the authority of the one now absent. The classic example of the man who marries a woman not to be his wife but to replace his mother is a tragic demonstration of this process. The marriage will endure only when the woman is as maladjusted as the man and willingly gives up the role of his wife in favor of that of his mother. Otherwise the marriage will dissolve when the woman concludes that the man is irredeemably locked into a neurotic dependency relationship with her that requires a responsibility on her part that is neither fair nor healthy. In her husband's case the child has not become father to the man; the man has remained a child.

It can be a heady experience to exercise authority over the lives of others. The taste of authority can be very sweet, and it can be addictive. It can also be a sedative against the pain of life that, left on its own without the authority over others that fills its days, would be without direction. Authority is sometimes a surrogate for self-worth, that is, it fills in the gap that exists whenever individuals cannot find purpose in relating to their own selves and so seek this purpose in an over-involved and over-influential relationship with others.

Power is the chief characteristic (and expression) of an authority that is described in this addictive and sedative fashion. This type of authority must always merit our close, specific, and attentive scrutiny, for it is here that we find the breeding ground of tyranny and the opposite of all prophetic authority, which exercises itself, as we said, not in power but persuasion. Power is built on the assumption that not all are equal in guiding their lives in a community; persuasion is built on just the opposite assumption. The prophetic life, in other words, recognizes the independent worth of human beings, the fact that no one has a right to *intrude* one's own convictions into the lives of others when they themselves possess other convictions, or no convictions at all.

This, I think, is the fundamental insight, the guiding thought that undergirds Ezekiel's great teaching on the autonomous responsibility of each individual to shape and follow his or her own conscience. What the prophet may do is assist in this shaping, attempting to form the consciences of others in a way consistent with his or her perception of God's will. But the prophet may not try to force this perception on others, to bludgeon them into an acceptance of it so that their consciences, no longer the result of their own free decisions, are not their own. For every individual, the prophet knows, has independent worth before the eyes of God, and every individual's convictions must be the result of a conscious and liberated choice. Otherwise the possibility is ever present that the integrity of the convictions is unjudged, their value unappraised, and their passion to drive the individual's life borrowed and always tentative.

When you have a wound you cannot heal, you know what it means to be powerless. The wound is a continual reminder that you are not in complete control of your life, that factors can intrude upon it, exercising an authority you cannot ignore. In the preceding chapter we described the prophet's experience of his call, his vocation, in just this fashion. But when all are prophets, when all are wounded by God in a way they cannot ignore, then all are equal. And the authority they exercise over each other can no longer be one of power, for that now belongs only to God, but one of persuasion. For what they seek from each other, what they need, is a convincing assessment of what their wound means, what its effects are at any given point in their lives. This assessment, however, cannot be legislated; it must be debated. It cannot be handed down; it must be brought up. It cannot be the responsibility of one or some; it is the responsibility of all. Prophetic authority, in short, can never be the breeding ground of human tyrannies. Before that could happen it would either kill itself or metamorphose into the mere exercise of power. No, what it helps bring to birth is not human tyranny but human community.

QUESTIONS FOR REFLECTION AND DISCUSSION

1. Since the word "authority" comes from a Greek verb meaning "to liberate" or "to set free," how have you experienced the exercise of authority in your life?

2. Should all human beings be considered equal in rights and privileges before each other and before God? If so, how does this affect a prophet's authority over us?

3. What do you ultimately prize more highly, security or freedom, being told what to do or having to decide it for yourself? What does your response mean when you assert that in some cases it is God who is doing the telling?

4. Which is the more effective way to exercise authority, through love or through fear?

5. Among the living community of Christians, and excluding the person of Jesus, who should exercise final authority within the community when determining the creed (what one believes), the code (how one behaves), and the cult (how one worships)?

CHAPTER FOUR

The Criticism

T he third trait of prophetic life, the criticism the prophet must practice, flows directly from the first two. Having been called by God, and having experienced the authority this call provides, the prophet must reveal to others the words of God. For like all revelation in the Old and New Testaments, the revelation to the prophets is never intended to be private, but is to be rehearsed before others because it involves them. God's call is a private experience only in the sense that it is delivered to just one individual; the authority is private only in the sense that the individual prophet alone possesses the words of God spoken to him or her. But this privacy offers us just an initial description of what has happened to the prophet. On a further description we become involved in what the prophet must *do* with what has been experienced: make it public. And what is made public, with the authority that the word of God provides, is frequently criticism of those with whom the prophet lives. Micah captures this characteristic of prophetic life when he proclaims before his listeners, "But I am full of strength, the spirit of the Lord, and of justice and power, to denounce his crime to Jacob and his sin to Israel" (Micah 3:8). Micah knows, as every prophet does, that his criticism derives from his double responsibility: first, to preach the word of God so that, second, it will influence the lives of others in a saving or redeeming way.

JUDGING WITH KNOWLEDGE AND PROPRIETY

No healthy individual likes to engage in the criticism of others. It is essentially a negative activity even when its final goal is a creative and uplifting one. For the first intent of criticism (at least of prophetic criticism) is to remove or destroy current or possible behavioral patterns that the critic finds unacceptable. Yet all of us, of course, also have a distressing knack for investing our pride of self in our present or anticipated behavior, which in turn often produces a rebound effect in us of varying degrees of harshness toward our critics. We want to "get even" with them, and we typically do this by criticizing something in their own present or anticipated behavior. A pendulum effect is produced, then, that keeps increasing the distance — the antipathy — between us and our critics. Finally, we may reach a point where we view the critic as a threat, an enemy to be overcome, and what may have once been mere irritation has become open hatred.

This "logic" of mutual criticism is particularly pathetic whenever the critics beforehand were friends, colleagues, or lovers. Countless marriages, for example, have dissolved under its influence. For criticism, we know, is more sharply felt the more intimately involved the critics are with each other. It can easily impress them as a breach of trust in a relationship that they believe should always be marked by a complete and unquestioning acceptance of each other. To criticize is seen as an attack on this spirit of acceptance, an assertion, in effect, that what one is can no longer be approved or tolerated. Why this might be so is perhaps discovered in the fact that within close or intimate relationships, where individuals have given themselves over completely to each other in love or friendship, any refusal of acceptance can readily be (and frequently is) understood as a refusal of the entire person. This can generate a concurrent response radical enough to turn even the deepest love into hatred, and to prove the ancient wisdom that the two, love and hate, are often twins in our relationships, now one, now the other, becoming alive and active.

The prophets are as aware as the rest of us of this "logic." They know that the criticism they must deliver holds the possibility of creating the intense hatred of others. This knowledge is perhaps nowhere more eloquently expressed than in the famous "Confessions" of Jeremiah (chapters 11-22, interspersed) where he describes himself at one point as "a man of strife and contention to the whole land" (15:10). We will see in Chapter Six that this is one of the reasons for their marked reluctance to pursue the prophetic life. Moreover, they are equally as aware of the fact (here unlike many of the rest of us) that they themselves are often guilty of the very things that they must criticize in others. This too, as we will see in Chapter 6, is a cause for their reluctance to pursue the prophetic life. No one likes to engage in activity that will immediately draw from others the accusation of hypocrisy.

Well in advance of Jesus, but certainly including him in their midst, all the prophets of the Old Testament know the meaning of his observation when they must criticize others: "Jerusalem! Jerusalem! You who stone the prophets and kill those who are sent to you" (Luke 13:34). The killing can be literal, the death of the prophet through brutalizing punishment. Or it can be figurative, the death of the prophet's reputation through the mocking charge of hypocrisy. In either case, people who were at first friendly toward the prophet, or at least pleasantly indifferent, become openly hostile and, in some instances (as the legendary *Martyrdom of Isaiah* testifies), even murderous.

The "logic" that turns love into hate, that makes antagonists out of friends and enemies out of lovers, was no stranger to the prophets. This logic can even seduce the prophet ("If they are going to treat me so unfairly, I will treat them the same way"), which Jesus, I think, is trying to offset in his renowned counsel, "Love your enemies, pray for those who persecute you." When the prophet's love and friendship toward others becomes challenged by their contempt and scorn for the criticism given, the prophet must not give in to the temptation to respond with a similar contempt and scorn. Rather, the prophet must double and re-double his or her love until it is no longer threatened by spite or the need to "get even," and continue to offer the criticism.

The prophets, then, persist in their criticism, no matter how strong their desire to abandon it. Under the impulse of God's call, the demand of their vocation, they preach God's word with an authority they cannot deny. Whatever frustration it might bring their way, they accept. Whatever contempt might greet them, they endure. Whatever pain might arise, they suffer. But they do none of these things from personal merit, just as they do not offer their criticism from personal desire. They have been wounded by God in a way they can neither heal nor forget, and the wound drives them to activity they would otherwise never perform.

When Jesus tread the road to Calvary, suffering the fate of his criticism, it was not a destiny he had planned or desired. Jesus was no masochist, no fool unaware of the consequences of his activity, as Neitzsche and others have argued. He was a God-driven man, a faithful man who preached what few wanted to hear and most were glad to be rid of by crucifying him into silence. On the way to Calvary, Jesus might have thought of the years he could have enjoyed, the seasons of a contented life and a peaceful death — were it not for the call of his God, the authority it gave him, and the message he had to preach. All his desires meant nothing before the persuasiveness of God acting in his life, calling him, and the conviction he shaped from this regarding what he must do.

This is passion we are talking about, the trusting power that drives individuals to perform tasks and teach lessons, to go distances and confront situations they would otherwise never perform and teach, go and confront. Its source is thus to be found outside the individual — something that enters into or is given to him or her — and religiously is described in terms like spirit, grace, blessing, God, and so on. Jesus engaged his public ministry, in other words, including the criticism it involved, not from self-motivation but from a passion he could not deny because he could not deny its source in his Father's will.

THE OBJECTS OF CRITICISM

The objects of the prophet's criticism can vary, though for the sake of convenience we can reduce them down to four general categories: 1) a specific individual, 2) a general population for either 3) a specific deed or 4) a general attitude. In any given instance, these categories can mix with one another.

1. *Criticism of an individual.* This criticism will usually involve someone with authority in the community. For the Old Testament prophets, of course, this is typically the king. The operative presumption in this category is that individuals who possess authority merit a closer scrutiny than those who do not. The person who has the right, for example, to send others into battle where they may lose their lives must be more closely assessed regarding the rectitude and wisdom of his behavioral motivations than the one who does not. The teacher who is charged with the moral education of children must be held more accountable for his or her behavior than those who are not.

The acceptance of authority simultaneously means openness to critical appraisal of one's activity; and the greater the authority, the greater the critical appraisal will amd must be. That is why the complaint frequently heard from those in authority — "People don't leave me alone." "People are forever on my back" — always rings a note of petulance that we can hope is only passing. People have a right to engage in a continuing critical assessment of those with authority over them. It is the same right that two people in love also possess over each other, since in its own fashion love too gives one person authority over another.

Or again: The prophet will always stand against the claim of anyone to possess an unquestionable authority on the basis of personal merit or privilege. The prophet will unerringly judge this claim, whether in the family, the school, the church, the nation, as an attempt to usurp a prerogative that belongs only to God, and so as a refusal of the humility that goes hand in hand with creatureliness.

2. *Criticism of a general population.* All prophets discover that preaching the message revealed to them often means they must criticize not only an individual but a group. In the Old Testament, of course, this is nearly always the community of Israel (or large portions of it) but sometimes other communities as well (we can think of the Assyrians, or more notably, the Babylonians). In the New Testament it would include such populations as "the Scribes and Pharisees" or those Jesus refers to more obliquely as "the men of this world." The prophets perceive that the group under consideration has departed in its behavior from acceptable norms laid out in the revelation of God's will. They rise up, therefore, and speak their criticism, risking the hatred or ridicule of the group.

The tenuousness of their situation, they know, is much greater here than when they must criticize an individual, even when that individual is a king. For they know what we all know, that the hatred or ridicule of a single individual can become compounded many times over when a mass of people responds as a single unit. The response of a single person to what angers him or her is often far more extreme when you place that person in a group of others who have been similarly irritated or angered. While someone might never stone to death an adulterous woman, the same person will do so if others will participate in throwing the stones. While someone alone might not kill a criticizing prophet, the same person will contribute to the murder in concert with others.

Conversely, of course, the virtue of individuals is also frequently strengthened in a group. When Peter defends his Lord before the soldiers in Gethsemane he is no doubt buoyed in his act by the presence of the other disciples. But when he is alone in the court-yard and must confess his discipleship while Jesus is on trial, he becomes a coward. Both virtue and vice are more easily practiced when you are the member of a group or community practicing the same. When you are not, when you must criticize the lack of virtue in a community that excuses or justifies its vice, every prophet must be prepared for the contempt and anger of others.

3. *Criticism for a specific deed.* The attention of prophetic criticism is often concentrated on a single act (or a series of similar single acts) that an individual or group has committed. The criticism here is isolating: it does not have repercussions on the rest of the individual's or group's activity. When Nathan criticizes David for the king's adultery, the criticism is directed only at the one specified act. It does not imply that David is continually an adulterous man. The prophet's perspective, in other words, is a limited one, and in the course of offering criticism he or she must make it clear that the implications of the criticism do not extend beyond their proper context. Nathan succeeds at this, of course. David understands that the prophet is not engaging in the classic error of all inductive thinking; he is not trying to make a particular example universally applicable. If he had, the criticism would not have succeeded. For although David knows his specific deed was wrong, he also knows that he has not thereby proved himself an adulterous man in general.

Nathan's sensitivity to what his task is in this particular situation obviously provides a worthy lesson to all who would engage the third characteristic of prophetic life. Thus the petulant husband (if I may here offer a commonplace example) who allows his wife's single misdeed to become the catalyst for a condemnation of her entire person is demonstrating a failure to appreciate the prophet's lesson, and in the process certainly not assisting his wife. For he has permitted the single misdeed to brood in his mind and to trigger ridiculous relationships to other deeds she has committed, until the one misdeed is judged as simply an instance of a whole way of life. The wife is defenseless before this onslaught of non-sequiturs, and what may have initially been a legitimate criticism of her becomes ludicrous in having to bear a meaning about her character as a whole, which it clearly does not possess. Her response can be patient acceptance of his unfairness, anger toward it, indifference or depression. But in no case will she find it a cause of her improvement. Above all, the third characteristic of prophetic living teaches us never to give our criticism a compass, or importance, it does not deserve.

4. *Criticism of a general attitude.* If the previous category of prophetic criticism had as its object a specific deed, this one has as its object a frame of mind, a manner or way of thinking. When a group or individual, for example, habitually demonstrates a behavior pattern in conflict with the word of God, the prophet will direct criticism not first at the deeds but at the attitude generating them. During the Exodus, Moses knows that his primary attention must be given not to all the complaining and despairing acts the people commit but to the underlying attitude of infidelity that brings them forward. So too Jesus addresses his uncompromising criticism of the Pharisees not first to specific fallacies in their behavior but to the attitude of self-righteousness they have nourished in their hearts and minds.

Through objection, personal example, a realistic analysis of past, present, and possible future situations, all prophets will attempt in any way possible to lure an attitude gone awry into a more intimate alignment with God's will. They are not always successful in this, just as they are not always successful in their criticism of specific deeds. But success, after all, is not their dominant concern; it is, rather, their intent to remain true to the tasks and authority their God has called them to. While they are aware that in developing patterns of behavior appropriate to God's will their fundamental task is to shape the attitudes of people, their ways of thinking, the prophets know that all they can do is assist in this shaping; they cannot force it, like some wraith crawling into people's minds and arranging or re-arranging their thoughts.

The prophet would understand (as many Christians have not) that when Jesus speaks about "sinning in your heart" he means that any consistent entertainment of a particular action in your mind will more often than not lead to that action whenever the proper opportunity arises. But all the prophet can do is point this out, diligently and without reserve; the prophet cannot control people's hearts, nor how they use the opportunities that lie before them. People must do these things for themselves. Whether they do or not, however, the prophet has at least been true to what he or she perceives is the will of God and the criticism of others this frequently involves.

Because of the call and authority they possess, Christians too, like the prophets of old, must willingly engage the task of a critical witness to the revelation of God's will they affirm. They must preach against anyone who in any way denies, ignores, or demeans this revelation. We can, therefore, perhaps best describe this third prophetic trait characterizing Christian life by speaking of the "shock therapy" that Christians must administer to others (again, to an individual or a group, for a specific deed or a general attitude) whenever the revelation they affirm is offended. Sometimes this therapy will be passive: By the way they live together, the example they give in their common life, Christians must offer positive if indirect witness to others of the revelation they affirm. Sometimes, on the other hand, this therapy will be active: Christians must extend themselves beyond their own communities, go out "into the world" and offer a positive and direct witness to others of the revelation they affirm.

Of these two forms of therapy, the first posseses an obvious primacy. Christians cannot effectively witness to those outside their communities when the witness they give within their communities makes a mockery of the revelation they affirm. Common sense alone will tell them that if you are preaching unqualified forgiveness or generosity or truthfulness to others, and yet in your own life are not practicing what you preach, you leave yourself open to justified derision. If it is clear to all that your own forgiveness is laced with condescension, your generosity with pride, your truthfulness with arrogance — or if you practice any of these virtues from mere convenience or expediency — how will you witness effectively to them before others? You will not. They will see quickly enough that while you expect them to practice these virtues without qualification toward you, you are not willing to reciprocate. The sham of your preaching will be exposed and your witness will be greeted with untempered ridicule or indifference.

What these remarks mean is that the criticism Christians exercise as a result of their calling must first be directed toward themselves. They must practice the therapy captured in the venerable adage "Physician, heal thyself" before they direct their attention toward healing others. For this practice has immediate effects on the mission mandated by Jesus in his final words recorded in the synoptic gospels and the book of Acts. Jesus says, in the Matthean rendition (28:19-20), "Go therefore and make disciples of all nations, baptizing them in the name of the Father and of the Son and of the Holy Spirit, teaching them to observe all that I have commanded you." But the baptizing and teaching of the disciples, their fidelity to the words of God expressed in the words of Jesus, can never succeed unless they first demonstrate "to the nations" how baptized and well-taught Christians live with each other. Yet, before they can do even this, or at least do it with integrity, they must engage in self-critical appraisal. The final concern of Christians, in other words, must always be an extroverted or "out-turning" one toward others, but their initial concern must be an introverted or "in-turning" toward themselves. We must understand that preaching the message of Jesus not only places us in an external relationship with those who are not Christians, but also in an internal relationship among ourselves who are.

If the Christian community can indeed be described as the body of Christ (according to Pauline teaching), then the first task of Christians is to make themselves, this body, something beautiful in the sight of others, something that attracts them and into which they will want to be incorporated, "enfleshed." An ugly, unattractive, repugnant Christian community, a community that has abused and failed to respect itself, just like any body that has been abused and shown disrespect by the person whose body it is, will only succeed in driving people away in disgust or drawing pity from them.

THE ART OF CRITICISM

Webster's defines criticism as "the art of judging with knowledge and propriety moral or logical values." The definition is an excellent one. Citicism is indeed an art. It is something that requires reflection and discretion, a delicacy of mind and heart that pursues its task "with knowledge and propriety." Criticism that is blurted out as a spontaneous response to some offense we find in ourselves or others will rarely have a beneficial effect. In these instances what we are expressing is better described as anger or resentment or disillusionment. Our response is functioning more as a "release mechanism," in other words, a freeing of emotions turning back on themselves that we cannot contain, rather than as a constructive appraisal of the offense.

We may note, of course, that at times this release of emotions is a healthy response to a situation we find unbearable; and the prophets often demonstrate it in their own lives. But it defines neither the spirit nor the intent of the critricism they engage in, which is noted not for its spontaneity but its well-honed and incisive reflectiveness, or as we described this in the preceding chapter, its obedience.

When prophetic criticism is effective, it is the product of prayer and reflection, study, and an objective assessment of the facts. It does not leap into the prophet's mind and then out his or her mouth without any activity in-between. Nor is it delivered with a whine or a pout, a spirit of "hurt feelings" that diminishes or destroys its value. Rather, it is delivered robustly and unmistakenly, without the ambiguity that it is merely reflecting the prophet's personal and disturbed opinions. Like the call and the authority, the prophet's criticism is untempered in its expressions. But guiding this untemperedness is the elemental concern to be persuasive when speaking of his or her call, the authority it provides, and the criticism it requires.

The definition above also gives us another clue to the character of prophetic criticism. According to it, the motivation for the criticism is judgment, which, as we typically understand this in the context of criticism, will mean something like censure or blame. There is no doubt that this is a legitimate understanding, and that it frequently describes the criticism the prophets engage in. They are masters of the diatribe, the passion-filled and censoring appraisal of the deeds and attitudes of others. It is while they are exercising this purpose of their criticism, in fact, that our usual pictoriography of them arises: lean, wild-eyed ascetics who mesmerize us with the intensity of their proclamation. We think of old paintings and recent films, literature that has made the prophets awesome in their untempered feelings, their drivenness in preaching God's word. They can become for us Jekyl-Hyde figures, people we respect yet at the same time fear.

If we were correct in Chapter One, it is their enthusiasm that does this to us, their "in-Godness," our impression that their criticism, while condemning, is also holy. We stand before them knowing that it is a human voice we hear, but with the eerie feeling that within it there also courses the voice of God. And so it is, therefore, that someone like Jeremiah indeed becomes a prophet for us and not merely an unhappy runaway from an old priestly family, or Amos a prophet and not a malcontent temporarily out of work, or Isaiah a prophet and not an angry old man running naked through the streets, or Ezekiel a prophet and not an exile-crazed hysteric whose preaching serves only to amuse or irritate his fellow captives.

In each case, negative judgment on these individuals is suspended by the perception that while they are not pretty, well-bred, or even well-mannered individuals, they possess within them, their words and actions, an authority that begs, or more frequently, commands us to listen. We know they are ignored only at the peril of our own development, our appreciation for what God's will is in the world.

Part of the effectiveness of the prophets' censure was no doubt due to the freedom they employed in describing the destiny of the unrepentant wrongdoer. Though it reaches its most exquisite form in apocalyptic spirituality (where it even includes stunning descriptions of the post-mortem destiny of the damned in Gehenna and the blessed in Paradise, descriptions absent in pre-apocalyptic prophetic spirituality), all the prophets are nonetheless aware of the pedagogical usefulness of portraying the inevitable peace of a life faithful to God's will and the inevitable turmoil of a life unfaithful to it. It is these portrayals that often give their criticism its bite.

The operative recognition here is that human beings will take more seriously criticism that relates directly to the quality of their life as a whole than criticism whose effects are confined to a given portion of it. If a prophet promises drought for the coming year because of some wrongdoing a person or people has committed, it is far less effective than if an entire lifetime of misery is promised. And the primary interest of all the prophets, as we have said, is precisely this effectiveness of what they are saying, the criticism they offer, and its ability to alter behavior. At times we may even have the impression that they will go to any extreme in their preaching to secure this alteration, and our judgment on the validity or humanity of their depictions of the sinner's (or saint's) destiny calls for reassessment. This is a fair impression, as long as we keep in mind that the principal intent of the prophets is not to elucidate the merited joys or pains of life but to employ whatever arguments they can to persuade people that their criticism is worthy of serious consideration.

There is a need to discriminate between the content of the prophet's teaching and the form employed to convey this content. Although we may agree with the content (e.g., that life should manifest obedience to God's will) we may not agree with the form in which it is expressed (e.g., promises of perdition or pleasure, pain or happiness to motivate an appreciation of the content). We must attend to the words of the prophets, to be sure; but we must do so with discretion. We must distinguish the word of God they preach (their prophecy in the strict sense) from their own ways of utilizing it pastorally or apologetically. This, after all, is to do nothing more than to practice the same freedom toward their words that they practice in their own fashion toward the words of others.

In much of the spirituality we read today there is a peculiar absence of the freedom the prophets practice in persuading people of the worthiness of their criticism. These spiritual writings have a tendency to isolate from other concerns of life the way we relate to God, and then to develop a limited "geography" of sources from which they try to draw their persuasion. Certain ideas and experiences are not considered appropriate areas for discussing what we call "relating to God." Good taste begins to prevail as a guideline in how arguments are structured; cultured biases become determining factors regarding what is said and how it is said. For we are afraid of alienating others, that by smashing the compartment in which they have placed the acceptable components involved in discussing "relating to God," they will turn a deaf ear to us altogether, in disgust or derision.

In all this, however, we show ourselves the reluctant heirs of the prophets, who, while not impervious to the scorn or derision of others, did not allow it to abridge their untempered passion to preach God's word in any and every way, freely roaming over the whole geography of human existence to seek their inspiration. They knew that alienating their listeners was a risk they had to take. But their constant hope was that somehow they would finally tap a responsive chord that would overcome this alienation and make their listeners attentive to the criticism.

Like the prophets before him, Jesus also censured those around him. And like the prophets too, he practiced a freedom allowing him to draw from whatever sources were available as the inspiration for this criticism. Anyone can see this in the amazing creativity, the "expansive creativity" in Charles Peguy's words, with which he set forth his parables and discourses. What Jesus knew, like every prophet, was that there is no forbidden terrain in the geography of human living that should not be explored for its potential service to the proclamation of God's word. Harlots and mustard seeds, whitewashed tombs and bodily functions, taxes and teaching rabbis: Jesus looked everywhere, at all the wrinkles that define the fabric of human experience to locate whatever was of use to him in the message he spoke. The word of God had to be made effective in human speech; criticizing human error had to strike home. The risk of alienating others had to be taken in the final hope of helping people — even if it meant, before the help came, being bracketted on a tree.

Jesus is a paradigm for the Christian prophet, then, not because he succeeded at his tasks (by any objective standard at the time, he was a failure) but because of his untempered striving to meet them in fidelity to his vocation. In fact, it is in just this striving that I think we can locate the source not only of his prophetic character but also of his blessedness, and so the blessedness of every faithful Christian. This blessedness, standing worthy before the eyes of God, is not a result of the achievement of a goal but of the passion we invest in striving for it. The goals that Jesus himself presents to us, for example, the ideals we are required to acknowledge in our behavior (e.g., an unqualified spirit of forgiveness, generosity, patience) can never be achieved or possessed like a commodity. For there will always be points in our lives where we depart from them, where we deny these ideals. But this cannot be what is important; if it were, we would be dealing with a man who is asking us to achieve the impossible, and then sets this achievement up as the criterion for God's blessing.

Rather, what is important is not the achievement of the goal but the degree to which we allow it to influence our lives, that is, the degree to which we strive for it, acknowledging all the while that we can never gain it completely. Our blessing, in short, is in our striving. And this applies not only to the types of goals mentioned above, but to the task of criticism that accompanies all prophetic living. It is not whether our criticism succeeds that makes us prophets, but our fidelity in pursuing it because we are seeking to work God's will in the world.

There is another function of prophetic criticism we must also note before closing this section. Just as there is criticism whose purpose is censure, so there is criticism whose purpose is consolation. The prophets are intent not only on placing blame where it rightly belongs, but in offering encouragement and strength where it is needed. The wild-eyed ascetic who speaks fearful things of the offenses we have committed against God's will gives way to the gentle, revivifying voice of the prophet who tells us consoling things.

We often forget this second task of prophetic criticism, perhaps because we are more struck by a loud than a quiet passion. Or perhaps it is because of what we said earlier, that we too readily equate criticism with censure, a destructive rather than an upbuilding experience. But the definition that has guided us these last few pages makes no such identification; it leaves open the possibility of another form of criticism, the intent of which is no longer to point a finger of blame but to embrace with open arms the weary and overwrought, the worn out who seek to do not too little but more than they can in living out God's will.

In this case scrupulosity has crept into their minds and hearts, the eternal suspicion that they are not accomplishing enough, not nearly enough, to acquit their fidelity to God's will. And this scrupulosity, the prophet knows, is demonic because it can kill even the strongest passion, the most committed striving of the individual. It does this through the despair it creates. Not feeling that one's passion is fruitful or one's striving blessed, always aware that one could be doing more in service to God's will, the individual finally comes to a point where he or she abandons passion and striving altogether. Life is hopeless, this person thinks, because he or she has fallen into the trap of viewing commitment according to the "commodity" ethic we described earlier. This person concentrates on the quantitative rather than the qualitative meaning of commitment to do God's will in the world. And in doing this, like anyone who does the same, all he or she can see are personal failures.

The prophets' criticism in the instances above will center around an encouragement of a greater trust in God's activity in the world. They will counsel a more ready willingness to place oneself in the hands of God, a confidence that God can work his will without the intervention of human agents. At the same time they will mellow this criticism with a prohibition against presumption. They will assert that while we can trust in God to work his will in the world, and that the realization of this will is not inherently dependent upon human works, we are still not exempt from partnering ourselves with God in this task. What the prophets want to avoid, in other words, is the seduction of either one of two opposing viewpoints. The one says that we need to do everything to secure the day when God's will is fully expressed in human living; the other says that we need to do nothing, that God will do all that is required. What is needed instead is a balance, the awareness that we must contribute whatever we can to the tasks set before us by God's word, but that whatever we contribute, it can only be partial. To complete the task we must rely on God's own good will, a reliance the prophets otherwise call hope.

A similar awareness, we may note, also forms a crucial part of the whole complex of meaning that surrounds the famed emphasis in prophetic spirituality on the future as the place where God will act — where God will do something new — in accomplishing his will. For even when the word of the prophet must bring affliction for his contemporaries, when it is a menacing force in their lives, it is more often than not accompanied by a statement of future redress from suffering, even justified suffering, and a consoling vision of the final realization of the relationship with them that God has initiated.

The prophet's criticism will thus have as its goal not only the creation of a legitimate sense of wrongdoing in individuals, but a strengthening of hope as well. The prophet will emphasize that one of the pre-eminent signs of a mature relationship with God is the recognition of one's limits, and that within this recognition there is a simultaneous awareness that we must not overestimate our ability in the tasks before us. In a contemporary idiom, the prophet will instruct us in what it means to "let go," to allow our limits to be filled out by others, especially by God, and to seek from them the help we need. And all this is done, as we said, to provide not censure but consolation. For there is indeed peace in knowing that in the tasks before us we are not going it alone, that we are partnered in our vocation, first with its source, the God who has called us, and then with all others he has similarly called. The tension that a sense of isolation causes, the feeling that I have no right or recourse to help in what I must do, thus dissolves in the consolation that solidarity and community always brings. In the next chapter, however, we will see that even this consolation is not an end in itself but brings forward the fourth trait of prophetic life, the political involvement that an awareness of community with others always demands.

LONELINESS

While the ultimate purpose of prophetic criticism is to unite people in a common recognition of the authority of God's will over their lives, the first (and sometimes only) result of prophetic preaching is often to disunite them, to cause discord in the community. Both Testaments are filled with sufficient examples of this phenomenon to make arguing it superfluous. Prophets frequently find that their criticism does not function symbolically but diabolically, that is, instead of drawing people together in a common vision or purpose (*symbolein*) it tears them apart, causing pain and an inability to communicate among them (*diabolein*).

In this situation the prophets of any culture may come to believe that all they have succeeded in creating is a tower of Babel in the hearts and minds of others, where isolation rather than communion describes their relationships. They may begin to think that all their efforts have gone for naught, that the controlling goal of their mission has gone blind, and that the only thing their criticism has thus succeeded in doing has been to drive a wedge between their clear perception of God's will and their ability to communicate this adequately to others.

At this point we can begin to appreciate the frustration that often plagues the prophets, a frustration they feel toward themselves for their inability at successful communication, and one they feel toward others for their lack of understanding or receptivity of what the prophets are saying. At this point, too, we can begin to appreciate the profound loneliness that often comes with prophetic criticism. We can begin to understand the stark confession of every prophet at some point, if only in the mind's privacy: "I am alone." It is a confession born from frustration, and it merits, I think, at least the following considerations in our attempt to understand better the meaning of prophetic living.

Loneliness is a harrowing state of mind. At an extreme, it is the experience of being walled off from one's surrounding world, its people, situations, and events. It creates a feeling of radical aloneness, of being unable to relate successfully to what is outside oneself, or of standing within a world that has lost its focus and become blurred, with no supports to give meaning and purpose to one's life. Loneliness is a state of mind wherein all paths of thought and feeling lead back to oneself; there appears no one and nothing, no source of consolation on which thought and feeling can anchor themselves. Like the self-consuming serpent that appears in folklore, thought and feeling become circular, always turning in on themselves. So does loneliness feed on itself, and thus, not drawing nourishment from another source, cannot become anything other than it is. That is why (following R.D. Laing's analysis) we should first define the autistic individual, the person who refuses to leave a fantasy world, where he or she plays an integral role in what is happening, for the real world where this role is absent, as a lonely individual.

If I may employ an example from the Old Testament with which many of the prophets were doubtlessly familiar and sympathetic: The plight of the unconsoled Job represents a particularly acute expression of the meaning of loneliness. Job possesses certain thoughts and feelings of the pain he is suffering. Yet, in no one can he find a receptive response to them. None of his friends understand his complaints, arguing instead that his thoughts and feelings, his assertions of innocence, are misguided. Job, they say, must have done something wrong to deserve his pain, even though he knows he has not. He must scour his memory in search of it, they say, even though he knows nothing will be found there. And his God is no comfort to him either, since he rightly perceives that it is by God's will that he is suffering in the first place. Everywhere he turns Job meets deaf or uncomprehending ears. Isolated with his thoughts and feelings from the people around him and the God within him, his loneliness is indeed complete and heart-rending. He is an island unto himself, confronting the pain of his existence.

A sense of isolation, then, of foreignness to one's surroundings, is the foremost mark of loneliness. It is like the experience of speaking a language that no one understands, or hearing one spoken that you don't understand. You become trapped in confusion, incommunicability. And the situation is one of pathos, suffering — not of a screaming, hysterical kind, but of a numbing, paralytic kind. Nothing you say or do appears to make any sense to others; it strikes no responsive chord in them, and you feel condemned and completely unaccepted.

This is exactly the situation, for example, of a man like Joseph K. in Kafka's haunting novel, *The Trial*. He is being tried for a crime that has never been explained, but which he is fairly certain he did not commit. Yet, he is unable to communicate his plight to anyone; his questions are either ignored or, when heard, misunderstood. He finds himself alone in an antagonistic world where the meanings of events and words make no sense to him, and his attempts to communicate this fact make no sense to others. He is living in a community where nothing he does seems right to others, where his criticisms are greeted with ridiculous smiles or contemptuous remarks. Joseph K. is a modern day Job, without the presence of God in his life. He represents on a larger scale what happens whenever two people, two lovers let us say, are no longer able to touch each other's hearts and minds, when a wall arises between them that prohibits the whispering, crying, even shouting messages they are trying to convey to each other. Joseph K., Job, and our two lovers have each been bricked into a world where they appear to be the only inhabitant, and each responds variously with fright, anger, frustration, depression, and resignation.

This situation Kierkegaard describes with the striking term, "shut-upness." Initially he intends the term to mean what Ernest Becker calls the "characterological lie," the phenomenon whereby individuals block off their perceptions of reality so as to create a closed self, not testing their powers in action, not exercising the freedom to discover themselves and their world in a relaxed way. In this sense, such individuals are themselves the agents of their isolation from those around them; they are the cause of their loneliness.

In an extended sense, however, I would suggest that the term could be equally well applied to situations like those of Job, Joseph K. and our two lovers above — and like that in which prophets frequently find themselves. Here our examples are not the agents of their shut-upness and isolation. Rather, these experiences are inflicted on them by others or by circumstances they have no control over. Their loneliness, then, is not self-induced but decreed, and they have little if any responsibility for it. Job, after all, like Isaiah and Jeremiah and Ezechiel, is not alone by his own will but by the will of others — which, of course, he cannot control (if we were correct at the close of the last chapter) but only seek to persuade. Job attempts this persuasion, we know, with a delicacy and precision of wit, a passion and rhetoric that makes his book one of the most profound in the Old Testament. But he fails. The wall he is trying to breach is too thick with the biases of an ancient theology, the prejudice of looking at events in only one way, and he cannot convince others that his suffering is undeserved. His cries of innocence thus echo around his solitary world, void of meaning for everyone but himself.

Whether self-induced or not, however, loneliness (aloneness, shut-upness) to some extent always marks the individual, in Colin Wilson's telling description, as an "outsider." As we said, such individuals feel in some fashion and to some degree unaccepted (or unacceptable) by others. At an extreme, they are like an undigestable bit of matter in the stomach that is expelled whole without contributing to the body's health and well-being. Whenever they reach out to others they cannot make contact; their hands close on empty air. They feel useless, a "useless passion" in Sartre's terms, unable to contribute to others or have others contribute to them. In short, between the lonely individual and other individuals there is a mutual lack of sympathy, of "suffering-with," that prohibits the frame of mind that the old meaning of "to suffer" tried to capture. "To suffer" is to allow; in our case to allow others to participate in your life, and in turn to be allowed to participate in theirs.

There are, of course, different degrees of loneliness. Very few individuals, including the prophets, would live in loneliness at its extreme degree. The sense of isolation and alienation we have described would, for a few, last day after day, year after year. Such an existence would be harrowing indeed; in most cases it would lead before long to mental breakdown and madness. The need to be accepted, that is, to be affirmed through successful relationships with others, is so important that lengthy, unredeemed loneliness would seem ineluctably to produce either 1) psychotic fantasies in which the real world is escaped in an imagined one, or 2) suicidal despair in which the real world is escaped in death. Either option functions, we could say, like the "release mechanism" earlier described. Only now, instead of liberating the individual from pent-up anger, he or she is liberated from a maddening loneliness.

As we said, most of us probably never experience loneliness to this extreme degree. In time it ordinarily dissipates. We experience lonely moments or even lonely days, but not a pervasive loneliness that lasts and stigmatizes our whole existence. Our loneliness is generally a restricted state of mind, a parenthesis in life otherwise marked by a reciprocity of meaning between ourselves and others. Loneliness comes and goes, in other words, and is often initiated and terminated by the most commonplace events. These events — for example, a harsh or consoling remark — can set in motion a whole series of thoughts and feelings that can either create or break our isolation. The event, whatever it might be, acts as a catalyst in imposing or diffusing a state of loneliness, and it is almost always unexpected and beyond our control.

Sartre is right, therefore, in his famous comment that "hell is other people." But he is only right when we interpret this to mean (which he does not) that we find ourselves in a world of men and women which does not accept us, with which we cannot communicate, in which we feel completely alone. Hell is other people only when we are isolated from them, utterly lonely, and knowing to the bone the truth of the saying: we all live in our own hells. So too, then, is Dante's portrait not only exquisitely wrought but profoundly correct in his great poem, The Inferno. There, in Dante's hell, no one is able to communicate effectively with anyone else in the sense of eliciting some semblance of meaning, purpose, or satisfaction from the other. All each can do is recite the story of his or her misdeeds and punishment to anyone who will listen, like a robot or recorder. A host of men and women live in Dante's hell, but each lives there alone, without sympathy or understanding from or for anyone else. And so Dante provides the best of our contemporary psychologists with an amazing portrait of what it means to be psychotically introverted, sociopathic insofar as the individual has withdrawn from human concourse because it is thought to be sterile, worthless.

The sociopath is not always someone who loathes other human beings and wishes them pain. Often the sociopath is someone who has become apathetic toward others because of the pain he or she has experienced through repeated failures to share anything of life with them. If the sociopath in some instances merits our fear, in other instances it is our pity. But in all instances he or she merits our attempts to understand and to heal.

Hell, then, is the state of not being accepted; in hell no one takes an interest in you. This, however, is not so much the result of an attitude of active hatred or scorn as it is of indifference. In hell everyone is indifferent to everyone else. There is, as we just said, no sympathetic bond between its inhabitants. Open contempt does not define relationships in hell; it is apathy. Each person is an autonomous being in the strictest sense. Human converse is at a standstill, and affection is dead. Hell is life in a hall of mirrors: Everywhere you turn you see only yourself reflected back. There is nothing new, nothing different in hell — no criticism because it would do no good. It is eternal isolation, existence in a lucite block. The fire that consumes the individual in hell is the fire of loneliness.

If we may describe hell in this way, then the correlate also seems clear: Redemption consists in overcoming loneliness. Again, this experience is common enough, occurring in a limited fashion whenever we are able to break through and communicate some idea or feeling to another which previously we could not. Or more seriously, it occurs whenever after many attempts we are able to find in another the acceptance of self we seek. In each of these instances we feel "redeemed" because our previous sense of isolation, of being unable to unite with another in sympathetic understanding, is overcome. Loneliness is dissolved whenever we can affirm that in some regard (our values, goals, work) we have been accepted by others, or at least one other. It is dissolved whenever we know that we have been heard and understood, that what we are, think, and feel *matters*. It is this moment of redemption, this moment of

sympathetic communicability, for which all prophets yearn when
they speak their criticism.

QUESTIONS FOR REFLECTION AND DISCUSSION

1. Does our culture and our church encourage prophetic criticism
    of each other?

2. If someone like Jeremiah (or for that matter, Jesus) were speaking
    to us today, would he say that the story of human history had
    gotten worse, was the same (history going around in circles),
    or had improved?

3. Implied throughout our remarks in this chapter is the idea that
    the fundamental *theological* criterion for the criticism of any
    value or proposition (for example, that there is a hell of
    everlasting damnation) is how you answer the inquiry, "What
    does it require me to say about God?" — and that if it requires
    me to say something about God I don't want to say, I deny the
    value or proposition. What do you think of this criterion?

4. We spoke briefly in this chapter of the need to accept others and
    be accepted by them, and then more extensively of the experience
    of loneliness when such acceptance does not occur. What does
    this acceptance involve from a prophetic viewpoint?

5. Stated throughout this chapter is the idea that among ourselves
    we will not tolerate certain types of behavior from each other;
    implied is the idea that any community has the right to remove
    from its membership a recalcitrant wrongdoer. But how would
    you respond to the theological inquiry, "Is there a type of
    behavior, a sin, that can place us completely outside *God's*
    mercy?"

CHAPTER FIVE

The Political Involvement

T he critical function, the third trait of prophetic life, leads to the fourth trait. Prophets know nothing of the distinction between church and state, religious life and civil life. For them there is only one standard governing human behaviour, namely, the revelation of God's will. When civil government offends this revelation, therefore, they consider it not only their right by their responsibility to become politically involved. One ony has to think here of the critical confrontations that a prophet like Nathan has with his king, David, or Isaiah with Ahaz, or Jeremiah with Zedekiah, or Jesus with Pilate and Herod. In each instance the prophet intrudes upon the political scene because he is convinced that the authority his call has given him, the demand of his vocation, requires that he preach God's will wherever this is needed.

AN ASSAULT ON INEQUITY AND IMMOBILITY

The advantage of the prophetic viewpoint in the task of structuring behavioral patterns is that it avoids a schizophrenic attitude in which the individual attempts to apply different values to different situations in life. We are all familiar with this attitude. It is what allows the businessman to practice a deceit in the office that he would never practice at home, a lack of forgiveness when dealing with his colleagues that he forbids himself when dealing with his children. It is the same attitude that allows the politician to spend unimagineable fortunes on apocalyptic weaponry designed to obliterate whole populations, while in her garden she wouldn't think of stepping on a bug; or to allocate funds for the on-demand abortion of human fetuses while she herself would go to any length to save her own unborn child.

There is a tension in these situations because there is a lack of wholeness, an absence of fluidity and integrity between one's actions. The individual is trying to compartmentalize life — and while in one compartment to pretend that the others do not exist. It is as if not one but many people were living one's life, all with different, sometimes contradictory values.

In its less extreme manifestation the result is what psychologists call a "functioning neurotic," that is, someone who is still capable of meeting basic responsibilities but does so with only a mechanical or unthinking grace. The functioning neurotic is caught in a conflict of values which steals meaning from life but does not completely incapacitate an ability to relate effectively with the surrounding world.

In its most extreme manifestation the result is the psychotic who has abandoned responsible behavior altogether. Unlike the functioning neurotic, in other words, the conflict of values the psychotic discovers in life not only robs it of meaning but also of the competence or aptitude to relate with any effectiveness at all to the surrounding world. Thus the psychotic either creates an imaginary world that explains (to an objective observer) his or her dysfunctional behavior, or withdraws into a state of mental (sometimes physical) catalepsy that produces no conscious or decisional activity whatsoever.

This disparity in behavioral patterns is greeted by the prophets with an alarmed concern. For they know that whenever values are in conflict with each other a vibration is set up within the mind and heart that may eventually tear an individual apart. They know that in this situation there can arise within a single personality warring elements that cannot always be arbitrated, and a process of fragmentation can begin that reduces the personality to a muddle (as with the functioning neurotic or psychotic just described). Unable to resolve the contradictions in their behavior, such people (to varying degrees) become incapable of making the proper choices to guide their lives. They are frightened that they will not apply in an intelligent way the prevailing values they bring to one situation as against another. Should the businessman really practice a deceit or ruthlessness in the business office that he would never practice in his home? Should the politician really support as public policy the pursuit of activities that she privately loathes?

Like a hungry animal caught equidistant between two sources of nourishment, they are unable to move because they want to move in different directions at the same time. And in this immobility they know with untarnished clarity the conundrum that faced Lot's wife. For she too desired to guide her life in two directions simultaneously— the direction of doing God's will in fleeing the city he condemned, and the direction of remaining there, at home, despite God's will — and in this conflict remains paralyzed to this day as a paradigm. The biblical narrative presents her metamorphosis into a pillar of salt as punishment for practicing a qualified submission to God's will. But perhaps, as we are suggesting, it can also be seen as an apt description of her inability to move when faced with opposing values, both of which she has made the mistake of nourishing in her life.

To resolve this tension, many individuals decide to give preference to one of the "compartments" of their life over the others. They conclude that they must apply a singular vision to guide life if they are to avoid the confusion or paralysis described above. But in the process, they know, some radical readjustments must occur in their behavior. Relationships with others must change, goals and dreams will have to be altered. The fragmentation in their values that before had allowed them to function effectively in a variety of situations, though inwardly it was tearing them apart, must be healed. And so the businessman begins to practice at home the same deceit he does in the office; or conversely, he refuses to practice at the office a deceit he does not practice at home. But while giving him the sense of wholeness he is seeking, the consequences of his decision are nonetheless clear and often severe. His home life dissolves because his family will not tolerate his deceit; it is a new experience of him they cannot accept because they cannot accommodate it to their understanding of love. Or his business life dissolves because his supervisors will not tolerate his honesty; it is a new experience of him they cannot accept because they cannot accommodate it to their understanding of competition.

In both cases the individual realizes that consistency of behavior is often purchased at the price of the antagonism of others. The uncompromising pursuit of one's convictions always has embedded in it the possibility of conflict with those who have different, incompatible convictions. This is the lesson, in its most extreme form, that every martyr teaches us. Between the martyr's convictions and those of his or her persecutors there is not only incompatibility but an open and killing hostility.

The prophet will sympathize with the procedure above for resolving a fragmented value system, but this sympathy is clothed in discretion. The prophet will say that in structuring a singular vision to guide your behavior you are not free to choose any vision you wish. Above all, you are not free to practice an expediency that selects a vision solely on the basis of its self-serving utility ("I will practice deceit and ruthlessness toward others whenever I can benefit by it"). To be sure, everyone needs a vision to guide life; it gives lucidity, clear-sightedness, and harmony to what one is doing and where one is going.

But for the prophet this vision is not created; it is provided. And the provision (the "offered vision") occurs in the words of God. Before the confusion of a fragmented consciousness, a divided life that has no direction because it has too many directions, the prophet will always point to the words of God calling the individual onto just one path, not many, the path of fidelity to the will revealed in the words. Yet, in the process of resolving the disparity in the individual's commitments, the values that guide life, it is this very fidelity that also requires political involvement.

As we said earlier, the will revealed in the words of God governs all patterns of human behavior, not just some, and the prophet must preach this will wherever it is needed. Subjection to God's will, in short, provides no options for the prophet. Either he or she submits entirely or, abandoning the integrity of faith, his or her convictions, submits selectively. The first option produces what we recognize as sanctity; the second produces what we will later describe as secularity.

The specifics of the political involvement of the prophet need not involve us here. In modern times as in ancient, the prophet must confront the idolatry, greed, and self-serving deceit of political leaders. The scenarios may have changed, but the plot is essentially the same. Whenever those in authority brutalize the revelation of God's will, the prophet must arise and speak against their sin, the calamity that human conceit, the refusal to abide even by God's will, always brings in its train. When wealth is unfairly hoarded, when food is not justly distributed, when the criminal accrues more rights than the victim, when the ill go untended, when the aged are treated like rotting meat — whenever any of these things occur in a community, the prophet must become politically involved and speak with an uncompromising voice to those in authority.

The prophet's voice becomes all the more urgent and the speaking the more critical whenever those in authority are themselves either passively or actively contributing to or sustaining these injustices. From the prophetic viewpoint, a community can never be asked fairly to tolerate in its political leaders indifference toward, let alone collusion in, the ills of the community, especially when these can be alleviated by the simple exercise of a responsible philanthropy. Not just a request but an untempered demand for justice will always roar from the prophet's mouth in this situation. This demand will reflect nothing of the expediency, the handy political casuistry that tries to bend itself around an uncomfortable issue with a thousand qualifications depriving it of its urgency or importance. Instead, the prophet's words will be direct, severe, unmistakeable in meaning, and imperative. This point is especially important for Christians to remember since so much of Christian piety has ignored or diminished the demands of political involvement. So much of the piety, that is, has forgotten that Jesus suffered two trials, one religious and the other political.

All true prophets speak words of liberation. They will preach the freedom of all men and women to live equitably with each other, that all are creatures of the same God, and that the privileges of some over others are humanly determined. What the prophets want is the unchaining of all who are enslaved to circumstances within human control that cause them to live less than equal to others. The freedom with which the prophets exercise the right to preach the word of God as effectively as they can is the same freedom that all must have to live as humanely as possible, which for the prophets means in accordance with God's guiding will. For they know that it is difficult to pray over God's word when you must worry about the roof over your head; they know that it is hard to put yourself into the task of caring for others when you are concerned about putting food into your stomach. The prophets' task, then, is to encourage a structuring of human relationships in such a way that there occurs the best possible context in which God's will can be served by all.

Yet, they also know that in this task the terrain of politics is a key ingredient, and that over it they must therefore journey with vigilant steps. It is in this political terrain that the hard, practical choices are made regarding how a community will organize itself, what priorities it will pursue, what values it will seek, what sacrifices it is willing to make for the sake of these values.

For in its initial phase of structuring an image of itself (including the religious–ethical components of the image) a community can act in any way it pleases. At this stage the image is essentially verbal and continually subject to refinement, argument, and contradiction; the work of structuring it is basically a mental exercise. But when the image begins to be applied politically, when it begins to influence the concrete behavior of the community — its laws governing the distribution of wealth, its treatment of criminals, the ill, the unborn, the aged, its education of children, its military posture, and so on — it ceases to be a mere mental construct and becomes functional in determining how people will live.

But prophets are not whimsical idealists spinning out dreams of utopia, a Never-Never Land where equality among people is simply wished into existence. They are realists driven by the untempered passion that God's will must be served, but that it can only be served when equity prevails regarding commonplace human needs: food, shelter, care in illness and age, time to think, time to play, to rest, and so on. As a result, they will not tolerate any human "gods" set up in disjunction to the will of the one God. They will require from these human "gods" an accounting for their pride, whose fundamental care must be directed not toward themselves but toward others, especially the deprived and suffering. As we said in Chapter Four, every prophet knows that there are some truths so compelling that they drag us to assent. One of these is that God's will cannot be served until we learn to serve each other; and that the more power you possess to perform this service, the more you are responsible for it.

THE SPIRIT OF SECULARITY

The political involvement of the prophets, of course, is not confined solely to their relationship with those who exercise authority within the community; it also includes relating to the community at large. What this specifically involves is an attentiveness to the way the community (not just its leaders) expresses its awareness of the responsibility that all possess before God's revealed will. What the prophets wish to secure, in other words, is that the political involvement they themselves practice is practiced by everyone. And they will be especially sensitive in this task to what in contemporary dress I would call the "spirit of secularity." This means the comfortable adjustment of religious convictions to prevailing cultural values when these are at odds with the individual's commitment to witness at all times and in all places to his or her convictions. In particular, the prophet recognizes that one of these places, a critical one, is the political arena, so that any withdrawal from it, any lack of concern in the arbitrations and policies of civil government — in brief, any refusal of the unconfined witness his or her commitment requires — represents a foreshortening of what any commitment to work God's will in the world means.

The person trapped in the spirit of secularity is thus similar to what Hegel describes as the "victim" in history. In both instances we are dealing with an individual who seeks to live a totally private life marked by personal happiness, while ignoring the movements of history as these are expressed in the surrounding world. This individual lives by a purely personal, expedient morality rather than by one directed toward bringing the reign of God's will toward actuality in the world. As a result, little or no attention is paid to the infidelity with which contemporary history greets this will. Both this individual and the prophet may therefore be crushed by this infidelity — by the intransigent wickedness human beings are capable of — but the victim is crushed by a deliberate blindness to this intransigence while the prophet is crushed fighting it in obedience to a conviction regarding what is good and right. If we were to attach moral value to their actions, then, we must inevitably value the prophet but not the victim because the former acts from an understanding of God's will which must be obeyed for the sake of establishing the benefit, the equality of all men and women, while the latter acts from a completely private morality and search for happiness that excludes concern for the morality and happiness of others.

It is one of the more popular pastimes of human consciousness to seek objects of blame for what is wrong in human behavior, particularly when we are considering our own behavior. If we are to believe the tradition expressed in the third chapter of Genesis, moreover, we must say that this pastime goes back to the very beginnings of human awareness. For when confronted by God with the wrong they have done, what do the man and woman, Adam and Eve, do? The man blames the woman for his behavior, the woman blames the serpent for hers, and the serpent, conveniently, has no one to blame. The intent of each of them, as is always the case with blame, is to provide an excuse absolving them from responsibility for their deeds.

Of course, we need hardly confine ourselves to the record of our Scriptures to justify the human proclivity for this pastime. We also see it written in the record of the early years of every man and woman's life. For what is the typical response of children when confronted with their misdeeds? Do they take fair responsibility for them? They do not. They point the finger of blame at someone else and start reciting their favorite litany when caught in wrongdoing, "It's not my fault, it's his"; "He made me do it. I didn't want to, but he made me," and so on.

We are not only familiar with these childish laments, we also have an uncanny ability for rehearsing them in more sophisticated forms throughout our entire lives. If we ask a war criminal to account for participation in the outrages that led to the mass extermination of whole populations of people, the bottom-line rationale will be, "I was only obeying orders. I did not make the decisions; I was only carrying them out in peril of my own life." We have here achieved no distance at all from the child's blunter response, "He made me do it."

Coursing through our existence, we discover more than ample evidence giving legitimacy to the behavioral heritage bequeathed us by the parents of the race. In our need to blame we are still the children we once were; in our need to excuse our wrongdoings by burdening others with it, we are each Adam, each Eve. And we only change when, like the serpent in Eden's garden, we find that we are alone before our wrongdoing; that there is no one left to blame, no excuses left that can remove responsibility from us.

We discover the dishonesty in every stance that seeks to establish our isolation from others when we are the objects of praise, while seeking communion with them when we are the objects of criticism. We understand the integrity that requires that if we are going to boast of our personal responsibility for the good we do, we must confess the same responsibility for the wrong we commit. When we apply the knife of moral judgment to our actions, it should cut first in only one direction, personal accountability. Otherwise, applied elsewhere, to the lives of others, we may discover one day that the mote we could have easily removed at first from our own eye has grown into a beam whose removal has become very difficult.

The prophets are keenly aware of this proclivity to shift responsibiltiy for our wrongdoing onto other shoulders. They are particularly sensitive to this when it comes to an assessment of political responsibility. It is not right to isolate out of the community those members charged with political authority and suggest that all failures in the political arena belong only to them. This is to practice a blaming spirit that seeks to excuse these failures as the responsibility of everyone.

If there is inequity in a society, if its political structures curry the increasing affluence of the wealthy and the growing poverty of the poor, if there is a crushing indifference to providing useful education, if there is persecution of any expression of religious fervor or delight, then the task of all prophets is to intervene personally and seek to alleviate the wrong they perceive. They cannot draw back from it, content that its responsibility belongs to others, and merely shake their heads at human perversity. To do so would make them equally as perverse, passive accomplices in the wrong done. In the classic terminology, what they would be guilty of is a sin of omission rather than commission, that is, a sin whose basis is not doing what they know they should, rather than doing what they know they should not.

In a Christian spirituality, this is the type of sin that will always meet the harshest condemnation, as when Jesus himself employs it as the basis for separating the good from the bad in the famous judgment narrative of Matthew 25 ("It was because I was hungry and you did not feed me, naked and you did not clothe me . . . .").

With these remarks we are back to the "spirit of secularity," previously mentioned. We described this as the comfortable adjustment of religious convictions to prevailing cultural values when these are at odds with the individual's commitment to witness at all times and in all places to his or her convictions. Or we could say: Of the two criteria for true prophecy that the Deuteronomist offers us — 1) its agreement with accepted perceptions of God's will (Deuteronomy 13:1-5) and 2) its agreement with empirical data (Deuteronomy 18:21-22) — the spirit of secularity is a clear offense against the first.

Or still again, but more briefly, we could say: The spirit of secularity is essentially immobile. It causes us to accept without critical judgment whatever circumstances define the "world" in which we live. Whether or not we agree with these circumstances makes no essential difference; we incorporate them as unassailable factors into our behavioral patterns. Our justification: "That's the way the world is."

The spirit of secularity knows nothing of the prophetic criticism described in the preceding chapter; it is eternally ready to applaud, or at least to greet with silent consent, the panorama of human inequities that surrounds it. At any rate, it does so until the individual in whom it dwells is also touched by these inequities. Then the cry, "Unfair!" will indeed bellow forth. But now, of course, it is a cry of conceit, unspoken until the individual is speaking for his or her own concerns.

The spirit of secularity dwells in each of us to some extent. Even the prophets of the Old Testament were not completely exempt from the way it can weave itself into our spirits. Their "confessions" are eloquent testimonies that they too were familiar with the desire to "let things remain the way they are." Even when Moses, the greatest of their number, was told of the oppression of his people in Egypt, he initially forswears the task of becoming politically involved that would eventually make him a prophet. His first response is one of negligence, a refusal of responsibility for others born of a satisfaction with what his life had become. The record doesn't say it exactly, but we may be sure that when confronted by his God with the task before him the spirit of secularity whispered something like this to Moses: "Tell God that his people in Egypt should free themselves; tell God that you are his good and obedient servant right where you are, that you need not become involved in other lives; tell God that you are content by his blessing and wish to remain so; *tell God to leave you alone."*

The spirit of secularity will always whisper the same resistance to God's will as did the serpent in Eden. It will taunt you with the idea that you have a right to carve out of your life whatever happiness you can, and that the needs of others are secondary. Like the demon in Goethe's *Faust*, it will hold before you the scenario of a life of personal contentment in which others are used, not assisted, by you. The spirit of secularity will insert as the repeating refrain into the song of your existence the idea that you have your own life to live and are not responsible for the lives of others. It will make you a child of Cain in mind and heart as surely as if you had been born in body from his loins. Like him, you will feel secure, even justified, in voicing this inquiry at your God, "Am I my brother's keeper?"

Some forms of spiritual immobility, of course, are beyond our control. Circumstances congregate in our life in a way that makes their power overwhelming. We discover that they have hedged us in, confined us with an authority we cannot resist. The child who has never known love will likely remain stuck in this lovelessness, unable to show love. The woman who has never been forgiven even her smallest faults by her husband may well remain paralyzed in her unforgiveness, unable to forgive others. The man who has relentlessly been taught to value the practice of greed may well remain frozen in his selfishness, unable to practice a willing generosity. In each case a spiritual immobility has been bred into the individual by others. And its strength is such that the counter-experiences can overcome it only if their strength is equally as potent. But these experiences, like those that caused the immobility, cannot be self-generated by the individual; they must be provided by others. The loveless child, the unforgiving woman, the greedy man left on their own will remain the way they are.

The prophets' attitude in the situation above will be one of great sympathy — an active sympathy designed to provide just the counter-experiences the individual needs to overcome his or her immobility. They will rage and threaten, cry and promise; they will speak with all the wit and persuasion they possess. But above all they will act, doing whatever is needed to contradict the cause of the individual's immobility. To the loveless child they will offer an abiding love; to the unforgiving woman they will practice a forgiveness that endures even after seventy times seven times; to the greedy they will show a generosity that gives continually more than was asked, a tunic as well as a cloak, a journey of two miles in place of one. The sympathy of the prophet is unbounded; it is fed on the desire to overcome all spiritual immobility that prohibits the individual from stirring from current ways of thinking and acting. Above all, the prophet is concerned with overcoming this immobility before the call of God. For when God calls it is always a call to act, to create, to serve in ways that require a mobility of mind and heart that is always ready to do God's will in any circumstance.

The immobility caused by the spirit of secularity, however, is not always uncontrollable. More frequently than not, it is chosen as a free option, the product of a conscious decision to live the way one does. And the criterion employed in the choice, what determines its direction, as already noted, is comfort. Those making this choice wish to slide through life with as few encumbrances as possible. They want their passions tamed by the times so that they will not emerge as different from others, a thorn in their community's side or a breach in their community's competency. They seek to melt even their strongest convictions into the values that surround them so that they will be, above all else, acceptable. And so, they turn their conscience away from all the blinding inequities that surround them, like they do their eyes from the blinding light of the noonday sun, because everyone else appears to be doing the very same thing. The spirit of secularity is essentially immobile because in faithfulness to it the individual chooses to be shaped by, rather than to shape, his or her surrounding world.

That is why it is only in populations imbued by this spirit that political tyrannies and the tyrants who create them can arise. Whenever you reduce your freedom to the point where you strive merely to reflect the lives of those around you, you have simultaneously abandoned your individuality, the possibility of offering a distinct and unique contribution to your community, and recklessly handed it over to those strong-willed who will take advantage of what you have done. Then the model you are effectively promoting for human community is that of the insect colony, where all the members remain basically indistinguishable from each other save for one creating agent, the queen. In harsher language, you are complying in the construction of a mass society, a congregation of mirror-imaged individuals whose differences are completely unimportant or tolerated as amusing eccentricities. This is the society that men like Nietzsche, Kierkegaard, Heidegger, and Marcel so bitterly and brilliantly condemn. Every prophet must do the same.

We see now that within a prophetic spirituality the responsibility for whatever social or political order prevails in a given community belongs not just to the community's leaders but to all its members. When something goes awry in the community's life, therefore, the finger that points in blame only at those in authority is the finger of the spirit of secularity. To this the prophet will always respond in untempered denial: It is not just the blame of those in authority; more basically, it is the blame of all because it is the responsibility of all. If there is a single thought that drives the prophet's political involvement, it is the conviction that each of us is responsible for rectifying whatever wrongs we find in the world around us, and to do so in whatever way we can. This thought could well be rehearsed in the minds of each of us as we too become aware of the inequities that exist in the world surrounding us. And as the thought begins to fructify into action, we will have the beginnings in our own life of the fourth characteristic of prophetic life.

FAILED GOALS

When you cast a cold eye on the tale of human history or simply examine the contemporary world around you, it is not difficult to understand how easily despair can slip into a human spirit. The panorama is one of extraordinary brutality, a meanness of mind that has led to guillotines, firing squads, holocausts, and hellish wars of incalculable ferocity. You become aware of the monstrous gap that has occurred in the development of animal consciousness which accounts for the willingness of human beings to kill the members of their own species. You see the depressing comedy in the realization that the dominant reason why members of other animal species slaughter each other, as a source of food, is one of the strongest taboos in the human species, the taboo against cannibalism. There is an abyss here in the development of the human species that no other animals have crossed, a pattern of consciousness that is singularly human and the cause of our demonic willingness to kill each other for countless reasons, unpracticed by any other creature. It is an unsettling gap that makes us qualitatively different from all other living forms. It is what we describe theologically as *sin*.

On a televised news program several months ago, the commentator appeared to be taking more delight in what he was saying the more lurid the particular news item was. He was most animated when he came to relay the guilty verdict passed on a young woman who five months previously had tortured her six-year-old son for several hours before finally taking him into the garage, putting his head in a vise and crushing the life out of him. The woman had not been judged insane upon psychiatric examination, and had shown no remorse for her behavior. Her one comment, repeated in a variety of ways, was that she had never wanted the child in the first place, that he had increasingly become an obstruction in her life, a threat to her plans and goals. So, she said, she "got rid of *it*," as if that six-year-old boy had become a useless piece of garbage.

Afterwards, an observer remarked, "It's no wonder that people commit suicide. Who wants to live in a world where even mothers kill their children, show no sorrow for it, and observers take only a mordant delight in the incident?" If I had tried to tell this observer of the political involvement required of the prophet, she would have only laughed at me, or sat in stunned amazement. All she could see in the world surrounding her, in the wickedness always lurking within human possibilities, was a cause for despair. Overwhelmed by the pessimism that can anticipate from the future only a repetition of the sins of the past and present, any political involvement whose purpose is to offer different possibilities for the future would have struck her as hopelessly naive, a wishful refusal of the way the world has always been and will remain. Humanity for her was graceless, corrupt, and demented in its self-consuming hatreds and conceits. There was no hope for lasting blessing or redemption among a race of creatures who had even managed to slaughter in a brutal act of stupidity the Jesus whose only offense was to offer what Whitehead calls "the brief Galilean vision of humility."

Despair is a continual temptation in the prophetic life. Whenever we give in to it, we give up our tasks because we realize that we are not all-powerful in life; that while we may possess the words of God, we do not share God's omnipotence. When we realize that we cannot do all we desire, we become melancholic; we withdraw from our desires entirely. We begin to think that what we are doing is without purpose, that our political involvement is pointless. The passions that have driven us — our faith, hope, and love — become sterile. We become poor in spirit in the negative sense, that is, our spirit becomes dull, weak, worn out. The desires that drove us, the commitments and enthusiasm that gave energy to our life, the mission we wished to accomplish — they all become meaningless.

Soon we may discover that the conflict that our failures have initiated in us, the conflict between our desires and our powerlessness to fulfill them, have not only impoverished but even murdered our spirit with despair. This despair is not necessarily, not even usually, the screaming, suicidal kind; it can be hidden very well. You might never see the poverty of spirit, the feelings of failure and frustration that give it birth. Despair is not always hysterical; it is often very quiet. But it is always untempered in the destruction it causes a human spirit.

The individual's spiritual life in this situation is characterized by what I call the three "A's". Let me conclude the remarks in this chapter with the following brief descriptions of each.

1. *Anarchy*. The word derives from the negative form of the Greek word *arche*, which means beginning or ideal in the sense of a motivating agent for thought or activity. Anarchy is thus a characteristic of despair insofar as despair is also experienced as psychological or spiritual paralysis, an inability to make a beginning, to move. Our experiences of failure can create this paralysis whenever we overstress the feeling of powerlessness these experiences involve. We give way to what I call the "seduction of the extreme," that is, we begin to feel that any of our desires, and any effort we make to fulfill them, will inevitably issue in failure and frustration. We commit the classic error of all inductive logic we referred to earlier by trying to make the knowledge we have gained from some experiences universally applicable.

Anarchy results in poverty of spirit in the negative sense because it deprives the individual of energizing motives, reasons for behaviour. Therefore, whenever you awake in the morning with nerves set on edge because there is nothing in the day ahead of you that makes getting out of bed any better an option than staying in it, you have had a small-scale experience of anarchy. On a larger scale, whenever there is *no* beckoning agent in your life at all, luring you into activity that is conscientiously engaged, activity that you *want* to perform, you are in the trap of anarchy. It is a petrifying existence in the strictest sense — the existence of an inanimate object which, unable to move by itself, can only be moved by something else — or what Sartre calls an existence of mere "being there," like a stone or park bench or clot of garbage on the ground. For the prophet it means that he or she no longer hears the call of God in life.

2. *Anomie*. Again, this word derives from the negative form of a Greek word, *nomos*, which means law or rubric or pattern of activity. Because we have no energizing motives for our behavior and exist in a state of anarchy, we can provide no framework to pattern our life on, no rubric for understanding it, no law for guiding it. Anomie is thus a characteristic of despair insofar as despair is also experienced as aimlessness in life, a going nowhere or a going around in circles. Without a law or rubric or pattern to shape our experiences, providing them with meaning and direction, we simply accumulate experiences, the way some of us might accumulate items in an attic. There is no relationship among them, nothing that ties them together. In short, they become absurd.

Upon reflection, this absurdity issues in the same paralyzing sense of importance that anarchy does. Therefore, whenever you awake in the morning with nerves set on edge, jump out of bed with a frantic rush of activity, and then realize that there is no rhyme or reason to what you are doing, you have had a small scale experience of anomie in your life. On a larger scale, it reduces you to a mindless cipher whose activity is engaged by sheer rote: You do the things "expected" of you, but do them with no satisfaction or sense of personal achievement. You become an automaton, a breathing, pulsing machine that lacks any self-generated meaning to its activity.

Having failed or unable to structure in your life any ideals (from *eidolon*, something pleasing or beautiful to behold which initiates your pursuit of it), you become trapped in anomie, possessing no rationale for personal judgment on how to think or what to do. Left on your own, your life then becomes hopelessly disorganized, and you become subject to the type of aesthetic existence described in Chapter 1: You live from moment to moment with nothing tying the moments together in a purposeful unity. For the prophet, it means that he or she can no longer exercise the authority a clear vision of purpose in life provides.

3. *Apathy.* Once again, this word derives from the negative form of a Greek word, *pathos*, which means passion, especially the sacrifice and suffering any true passion involves. Because we have no ideals (anarchy) with which to motivate a pattern of behavior (anomie), we become indifferent to life (apathy). Apathy is thus a characteristic of despair insofar as despair is also experienced as the absence of any interest able to elicit our commitment. Therefore, whenever you awake in the morning with nerves set on edge and think that you might as well be dead as alive, you have had a small scale experience of apathy in your life. On a larger scale, it forms an immediate prelude to flirtations with suicide. For now you find yourself confronted in harsh fashion with a question that wrestles itself into consciousness, no matter how hard you try to ignore it, "Is there really anything worth living for?" And to it, trapped in your apathy, your answer inevitably emerges as "No."

There is nothing really worth living for because there is nothing you can attach your passion to, your full-hearted and willing devotion, your enthusiasm as we said in Chapter Two. And so you remain stuck in indifference, neither loving nor hating the world around you and the life within you, but dead to each. For the prophet, it means that he or she can no longer see the purpose in practicing the criticism and political involvement that the call and its authority require. Like anarchy and anomie, therefore, apathy is a paralyzing, immobilizing experience. And with them it forms the triumvirate of attitudes whenever failure is allowed to issue in despair.

Despair, however, is only one stance we might take in the face of our failures. For there is a second stance, the one I call *humor*, which we might also take. Here we do not give up when we realize that we are not all-powerful in life. We do not become melancholic; we do not withdraw from our desires. Our spirit does not become weak, dull, worn out. We do not forsake our passions or the mission that gives them shape. Our faith, hope, love do not become sterile. Instead, when we realize that we cannot do all that we desire to do, our response is not despair but laughter.

Yet, we laugh not at some cruel fate or savage providence that gave us desires we cannot fulfill. Rather, we laugh at ourselves, at the very presumption that we could do by ourselves what we desire. And from this laughter, from the experience of failure that produced it, we learn like every true prophet does that our life is not entirely in our own hands but also in the hands of God. We learn trust in God, in other words, and from this trust, self-abandonment to God's guiding care. And we also learn that some of our desires, even when they are affiliated with our perception of God's will, are not by that fact assured of fulfillment; that when pursued to their end they may offer us not a taste of success but a taste of dust and ashes.

Finally, we learn that to be poor in spirit becomes a virtue, as Jesus taught, whenever it strips us of our conceit and makes us aware that we need help, the help of other human beings (if we are indeed to be politically involved) but ultimately the help of God. Only with this help do we have a chance of remaining faithful to, because we have found worth and value in, doing what we know we must do.

To be poor in spirit, then, as the prophets sought to be, to profess powerlessness as a way of life, means fundamentally to acknowledge that we need help and to accept this help when it is offered, expecially in healing those inequities within a community that any political involvement unveils. It is to assert without qualification that we must become brothers and sisters to each other's guidance and care. And for the Christian, of course, it is to confess that this can only mean, first and last, abandonment to the guidance of the witness of Jesus and the care of his ever-present Spirit.

QUESTIONS FOR REFLECTION AND DISCUSSION

1. If the will of God applies in all the dimensions of human existence, can we justify the notion of a separation between church and state?

2. Since the biblical prophets experienced nothing of democratic forms of government, what might their repsonse be to a political

system like that in America — for example, would they condone the politics of capitalism and would they give everyone the right to vote?

3. What might be the prophetic stance on political issues like conscientious objection to a war, the building and deployment of nuclear weapons, and what is needed in the human community to secure a lasting peace?

4. Throughout this chapter we dealt with the question of whether or not different values should be applied to different situations in life (for example, should deceit be an accepted, and even presumed, practice in diplomatic negotiations but never in the conversations between a wife and husband?). How would you respond to this question?

5. We described the experiences of anarchy, anomie, and apathy in this chapter as they can affect an individual. In your experience of Christians as a community, a church, do any of these descriptions apply?

CHAPTER SIX

The Reluctance

T he task of prophecy is not easy; countless passages in the books of the prophets attest poignantly to this. The prophetic life is difficult; nowhere in their writings do we catch the idea that the prophets thought it might issue in tranquility, the contentment of a life that has eased its way through the years without turmoil. From the moment they realize that God has called them, the prophets also realize that their lives are no longer their own. With the birth of their vocations there is born simultaneously the awareness that their lives now belong to another, without qualification or appeal. Yet, since no one wishes to give up his or her life completely, to place it entirely in the hands of another — even when this is God — we come at last to our fifth and final trait of prophetic life: the prophet's reluctance. Until self-concern was overcome in an often arduous and painful work of personal discipline, no prophet ever born, wanted to be a prophet. Even in those cases when the experience of the call was initially exciting, when the prophet felt chosen and secure in the blessing of God, he or she eventually sees this excitement dissipate in the rigor and sacrifice, the disenchantment and frustration to which this vocation inevitably leads.

Like the bliss that marks the beginnings of love, the sense of excitement and self-abandon we so accurately describe with the metaphor, "falling in love," so the prophet's calling can at first be a happy, almost thoughtless experience. But just like the love between two people when they have ceased "falling," get up and discover that the hard ground on which their love must survive includes not just bliss but work, not only happy but unhappy experiences, contentment as well as disappointment, so the prophet eventually discovers the same about his or her vocation. And with this discovery reluctance is born, nourished, and becomes full bred.

What might the specific causes of this reluctance be? We could allow our imaginations to nurture this question at length; roaming over the record of the lives and ministries of the prophets, we could determine countless answers to it. This procedure would undoubtedly have merit, for it would allow us to attend more thoroughly to reasons for the prophets' reluctance that closely match our own. This would give the prophetic witness an urgency and relevance it might otherwise not possess. If the contours of our own reluctance find closer parallels in Jeremiah than in Ezechial, for example, or in Hosea than in Amos, it is to these former prophets that we would then be free to go to seek an appreciation of why our own vocation to a prophetic life is uneasily approached.

For the purposes of this book, however, this procedure would be doomed from the start. I couldn't possibly isolate for notice, let alone discussion, the many reasons that any reader of the prophetic books might discover for understanding the prophets' reluctance to accept their vocation. The same comment, of course, could be made with equal legitimacy about the other four traits of prophetic life previously described. Any reader could undoubtedly fill out with a fuller meaning from his or her own life, experiences, and education, what I said about the call and authority of the prophet, the criticism and political involvement. All I could do was touch on characteristics that touched me, and to describe each in a way that made them part of any prophetic life, not just their specific applications in the lives of particular prophets.

My discussion throughout this book, in other words, has not been designed to provide an exhaustive analysis of each of the five traits of the prophetic life in all the complex detail each might involve in the life of any individual prophet. Even if this were my intent,

I'm not certain it would be well-advised because I'm not certain it would be possible. My intent, rather, has only been to offer a catalyst that might cause my readers to engage the works of individual prophets in a more thorough way than I have here, so that they will come to understand and appreciate that prophecy is an essential mark of any spirituality based on the Old Testament, including the spirituality taught by Jesus. Or as I noted in the preface, it is more an exhortative than an exegetical task I have set for myself. I am not presuming in the reader a familiar interest in the prophets. I am asking that he or she develop one.

AN UNEASY CALLING

What, then, are the descriptive characteristics of prophetic reluctance? I would name three: the fear of hypocrisy, the fear of physical abuse, and the disruptiveness his or her vocation causes in life.

1. *The fear of hypocrisy.* The prophets, sinners themselves, must often arise and accuse others of the very same sins they themselves are guilty of. The greedy one must accuse others of greed; the adulterer must speak against the adulterous neighbors; the arrogant citizen must confront the arrogant king; the self-righteous layman must offer recrimination against the self-righteous priest; and so on. But what will greet the prophets when they do these things, no matter how often they may proclaim their unworthiness to preach God's will and no matter how repugnant they may find their task, if not derision, mocking laughter, even hatred? For the witness of their own life gives ample encouragement to the accusation that they are preaching what they themselves have not practiced. It is too much, this discrepancy, and the listeners will consign what they have heard to the only place they believe it belongs: the prision of their contempt or indifference where it will have no effect on their lives.

Imagine how you yourself might feel, for example, if your neighbor, a notorious miser, began lecturing you on the merits of generosity and recommended a more thorough practice of it in your life; or if your business associate, a known and adept liar, started advising you on the absence of truthfulness she has noted in your behavior; or how would you respond if a professional colleague with a deserved reputation for brutality in his climb "to the top" reprimanded you for your own ambition? In each of these cases what the individual has said to you may be true; you may indeed be miserly or deceitful or ambitious. But your feelings, of course, are not being shaped by this awareness, but by the fact that the individual criticizing you is guilty many times over, or at least as equally as you, of the very same things.

This is the conundrum every prophet faces: knowing what your feelings will be when he or she must call you to account for the same wrongs for which his or her guilt is also manifest, even more manifest than yours. And it is this conundrum that makes the prophet reluctant.

But still the prophets persist, despite their reluctance, harrowed by a conscience that will not keep quiet and the voices of others telling them of their hypocrisy. The call, the authority it brings, the revelation, *not* their own life, which is the standard of their criticism, and the need to become involved in any facet of society to which this criticism may lead — all these demand persistence, the abandonment of any hesitating fear. There is a sense in which every prophet must continually repeat inwardly, if not aloud to others, "Don't do as I have done; do as I say." But this is not an assertion of pride, the conceit whereby someone proclaims freedom from the judgment of others. It is, rather, a confession of humility, the recognition that every prophet's life is also laced with sin, that it cannot provide an adequate criterion for behavior, but that the word of God must still be preached. When prophets speak their criticism, in other words, they are not always speaking just to others; frequently they are speaking to themselves as well. Their words constitute not only a colloquy but also a soliloquy; the audience they are addressing often includes themselves.

This is the phenomenon of conscience we see operating in the prophets, the interior voice that commands, accuses, consoles, or chastises us whenever we reflect seriously on our behaviour. It is the inner "wisdom" or guide described both by Jeremiah's insight that the law of God is written on our hearts and not on tablets of stone, and the insistence of someone like Jesus that every individual is personally responsible for what he or she does, that the individual cannot place this responsibility unfairly on other shoulders. Conscience is where we tend to relate most directly to God, therefore, and to ourselves. It is the "place" where we are most likely to practice an untempered honesty regarding our behavior because there are no human witnesses to what we are doing, and so no need to worry about our standing or reputation in their eyes. Unless we have allowed our pride of self to infest us so deeply that we cannot speak honestly even to ourselves, conscience is always the mother of humility.

Such humility makes the true prophets disctinct from the false prophets. The latter never admit their own wrongdoing and experience no reluctance whatever in criticizing the wrongdoing of others. In contemporary dress this is the "soap box" prophet who will stand on any street corner and scream self-righteous fury at any passerby, whether or not the passerby deserves the censure. For the presumption of the false prophets is that every human being is wrapped in sin, "perverse from the day you were born," and that it is their unquestioned right to point this out. Confronted by the true prophets they will hurl accusations of blasphemy: That the true prophets do not represent God because their reluctance is a brake upon their passion, a clear indication that the demonic is at work preventing full release to the power of God's word. The false prophets never fear hypocrisy in what they say because they are convinced that they have been chosen by God, and that their election automatically suspends any judgment they need make on their own life, its worthiness and sanctity.

Like some old metaphors regarding the effect of the sacraments, the false prophets believe that their "calling" has cleansed their past of all its sin and fault, that they are now one of the "perfect" or "elect," and that humility is no longer relevant to how they view themselves. They become what we described in an earlier chapter as religious maniacs, theological egotists whose self-image is braced by a fraudulent understanding of their relationship to God. The false prophets never direct their words of accusation against themselves; they never engage in soliloquies of self-recrimination; they never acknowledge their own sin, let alone that it might be greater than the sin of the people to whom they speak. Utterly convinced that they have been called by God in a way that makes them privileged above all other men and women, unaccountable before any judgment seat, the false prophets have allowed their conviction to kill their conscience.

What we are saying is that to the charge of hypocrisy, when legitimate, the true prophets willingly submit. They do not try to deny in the observations of others what they themselves know to be true.

Yet, this submission is not at the same time an abdication of their tasks. It does not lead them to paralysis but to humility, and a reappraisal of their role in what lies ahead of them. But this reappraisal does not overcome their reluctance completely but only manages to make it inoperative in shaping their *final* response to the call of their God and the authority, criticism, and political involvement this includes.

The true prophets know that in assessing their worthiness for the prophetic life it is only the judgment of God, not the judgment of others, not even their own judgment of themselves, that matters. But still these other judgments remain in their mind, influencing how they see the tasks ahead of them, the ridicule and contempt and indifference they may well draw from those they preach to. And so all true prophets still remain reluctant.

2. *The fear of physical abuse.* When confronted by an unpleasant situation, we have a tendency to become increasingly extreme in our responses to be rid of it. We find this expressed, for example, in the commonplace experience I call the "gadfly phenomenon." We all know what it is like to have a fly buzzing around our head. When it first begins our initial response is to dodge our head away from it; we want to consider the fly a minor nuisance that we can handle with as little energy as possible. But the fly persists, of course, and the nuisance it creates grows larger. So now we not only dodge our head but also try brushing it away with our hand. We hope that this further response will definitely discourage it from bothering us. But we fail. The fly not only continues to buzz around our head, but now seems to do so with even greater persistence. It is as if the fly were deliberately antagonizing us. And so our response becomes even more extreme. We start to hunt the fly. If it will not be discouraged by our lesser displays of irritation, we will simply eliminate it from our lives. We form the conscious purpose of smashing it out of existence. And we are intent enough on this purpose, the fly has antagonized us sufficiently, that we will carry out our intent no matter how much energy or time it takes. The fly has become an enemy that we can no longer tolerate, a disruption in our lives that we cannot accept.

In this whole process of thought, of course, we have abandoned our awareness that the fly is not deliberately antagonizing us, that it has formed no conscious motive to do what it can to draw our anger or fury. The fly is simply being itself, a creature of God we no longer respect. Yet, the disruption it has caused us is not seen in the context of its right to live or the unthinking compulsiveness of its behavior. All we sense is our increasing aggravation and the growing desire to be rid of its source. Only later, upon further reflection over the incident, might we realize that our behavior may have been as compulsive, as little expressive of intelligent and responsible thought, as the fly's.

The prophets, like the rest of us, are aware of such a behavioral phenomenon. And they are aware (like, from a different religious tradition, Socrates was) that in our example their role is like that of the fly, gadflies upon the hearts and minds of others. But their awareness is not a happy one; it does not produce contentment but reluctance toward the task ahead of them. They know that persistence in this task will draw increasingly extreme responses from those they are disturbing. Only initially will their listeners try to brush the prophets off as mere annoyances. If the disturbing behavior persists (as it will), they will make a more concerted effort to be rid of the prophets. And at this point they may well cease hurling invectives, accusations of pride and self-righteousness, and start hurling stones.

The fear the prophets have thus alters from one based on the desire to avoid hypocritical behavior to one based on the desire to avoid physical abuse, at its extreme, death. They become reluctant to engage the task of prophecy because it may well issue not only in character assassination but bodily assassination. And martyrdom to the cause of his God's will is not something they actively seek; in fact, it is something they much prefer to avoid.

Faced with such a situation, then, the question of the prophet is not, "What is the meaning of death; what does death hold for me?" but rather, "Is there anything I am willing to die for?" The prophetic perspective, in other words, is directed away from oneself, one's own curiosity or anxiety about death, toward discovering the existence of a cause one would sacrifice even life itself for. This is a difficult perspective to develop, of course, since it requires the individual to abdicate concern over questions that have perennially surrounded the anticipation of death: Questions of a soul separable from the body, reward and punishment, heaven and hell, and so on.

For the prophet, these questions can produce only idle musings if the individual has not first come to grips with the more fundamental question of whether or not there is a cause that can make his or her death worthwhile. For it is the answer to this question, the prophet knows, that will determine whether the reluctance to engage the prophetic life will be strengthened or overcome.

This is the same perspective, we may note (and the merit, in my view), of the philosophy of life that someone like Albert Camus also attempts to develop throughout his major works, especially *The Rebel*. Like the prophets, Camus is concerned with identifying a cause (in what for him, however, is a godless world) that if necessary will provide a sufficient motive for going to one's death. Throughout *The Rebel* he likewise reminds us of how this cause can have embedded within it the political involvement of the individual, though a similar reminder, we know, could be had just as easily by reading the prophets. Camus was called "the conscience of his generation," and this is a worthy acknowledgment of his efforts to examine critically the values that guide our lives. But the same description could just as legitimately be given to the prophets, all of them, any of them, in any age — to a Catherine of Siena, a Martin Luther King, Jr., a Mother Teresa of Calcutta.

It is not, therefore, that the prophet is indifferent to the question of death, as is sometimes alleged. It is that his or her assessment of the meaning of death is directly related to an assessment of the meaning of life. In other words, for the prophet, death in itself is an empty experience. Nothing can be said for it except that it provides the goal toward which life is heading and hence serves as the primary catalyst focusing the individual's attention on the meaning of life itself. In this viewpoint, the prophet is kin to many of our modern "existentialists" (as the above comments on Camus indicate), and a disinterested observer of the human obsession with what happens at the moment of death and afterwards. The prophet accepts without undue worry or curiosity the fact that the only death we observe is the death of others, and that they are always inarticulate about what they have experienced. No, the question of the meaning of death is not a value unto itself but only becomes valuable as it metamorphoses into the question of the meaning of life. And this question in turn has value only as it elicits an inquiry like, "Is there a cause in life I am willing to die for?"

The prophet's answer to this question has already been implied in the description we have given of the experience of the call. The enthusiasm we said this experience generates, the authority it provides to preach God's will in the world, is the sufficient basis shaping a cause the prophet would die for. The cause is doing God's will. Or more exactly put: It is fidelity to the conviction gained through obedience that God's will is known and must be preached, and that this preaching provides a higher standard of behavior than the preservation of one's life.

Yet, the same must also be said here as was said of the prophet's fear of hypocrisy. For one's awareness that there is a higher good one must be devoted to than the obvious good of preserving life does not automatically eliminate from consciousness the desire to preserve one's life. If the prophet refuses to "moralize" about death, in other words, to see it as the Grim Reaper bringing an end to a happy life or the Angel of Mercy terminating an unhappy one, this does not mean indifference to the question of continued existence after death. The refusal does not imply a truncated consciousness unaware that someday he or she will become a body sightless, breathless, mindless, dead. The prophet does not succumb to the childish idea so many adults carry with them long beyond their childhood years, the idea that causes children to acknowledge death intellectually but to act as if it will only happen to everyone else, not to them. Instead, the prophet is ever aware of death, all the more so because knowing that the way he or she lives, the way of the prophet, may hasten it more quickly than if he or she lived another way. And while it does not cause a refusal of this way of life, it does cause reluctance to engage it.

3. *The disruptiveness that the prophet's vocation brings into life.* Desires, plans, values, what one thinks one is or wishes to be, become subject to continual reassessment under the influence of God's call and the submission this demands of the prophet. The prophetic life is not comfortable or convenient. It does not issue in the security of selecting and pursuing one's own dreams and hopes. Instead, it requires an act of unqualified self-abandonment, the dispossession of the use of one's life for anything else than use by God. This self-abandonment obviously becomes the more difficult the more the lives of others are directly touched by one's own, but who themselves have not experienced God's call the way the prophet has.

Many of the prophets of the Old Testament, for example, had wives and children whom we may be sure did not understand the dispossession with which the man guided his life. Some may have remained faithful to him despite this, not understanding but at least accepting that he was compelled to live as he did. Others, however, neither understood nor accepted a way of life that was beyond the limits of their own experience. And in their refusal, of course, they immediately became living demonstrations of the naive faith that thinks God will never act except through our expectations. For the hard truth is that this is not so, a truth to which the prophets themselves are our fundamental witnesses. God's will is frequently intrusive in our life; it is unbidden, unexpected, and incommensurate with all our previous experiences. And those who refuse this truth, the prophets will say (even to their loved ones), those who think they can bind the will of God to comfortable or familiar experiences or expectations, are guilty of paganism. God's will is a devouring fire, says the prophet who wrote of Jesus to the Hebrews (12:29). And so it is. Its freedom is determined only by God.

Whenever we sanctify a certain image of our life and begin shepherding all our time and talents toward realizing this image, we simultaneously close ourselves off to other images, other uses of our time and talents. The more pride of self we have invested in the selected image, the more closely will we guard its realization in our life. In fact, we become imprisoned by the image until a point is reached where we are no longer controlling it, it is controlling us. The woman, for example, who has an image of life as it proceeds up the ladder of business success "to the top," may discover that in allowing this image to dominate her life she has missed much that would have been of value and beauty to her. I bring up this particular example simply because it is commonplace in our society. It indicates that our estimate of our capabilities — the way we understand the limits of what we can do to draw meaning for our lives — is frequently less generous than what our capabilities are.

The problem is that we often do not become aware of this until we are shocked into the awareness, which many times means when it is too late. What I am getting at in these remarks, in other words, is that just as there can arise within us a temptation to overestimate our limits, which leads to claims of an irresponsible self-esteem, so there can arise a temptation to underestimate our limits, which leads to claims of an irresponsible self-denigration. What we think we can be is open to one of two possible errors: The first occurs when we create an image of ourselves that exceeds our possibilities; the second occurs when we create an image of ourselves that foreshortens these possibilities. In either case, we have hemmed ourselves into a life that is fundamentally unrealistic because it fails to reflect an adequate evaluation of our talents, education, capacity for personal discipline, and so on. Although we might be happy living this way (with either one of the two errors), our life also lacks integrity. And this in turn (unless we have completely forsworn the critical function of conscience) must inevitably emerge in a painful self-appraisal of what we have done with our lives.

We may be sure that the prophets all had certain images of how they wished their lives to proceed. All had formed an estimation of their capabilities, and all intended to live out their years within the limits it imposed. But then all were shocked into the awareness — in their cases it did not come too late — that this estimation of what they could do was inaccurate; more, it was unacceptable. The shock came in the form of a call from God, a vocation that demanded the destruction of their old image of their lives, and the comfortable but insufficiently judged possibilities it held, and its replacement by a new image, that of a *prophetic* life. All that had been previously dreamt and hoped for in life, and the tranquility it produced by its familiarity, had to be abandoned. There would be no more personal dreams and hopes, no more satisfying limits within which life would be organized, no more self-created images to guide existence to a contented end.

But as with the fear of hypocrisy and the fear of physical abuse, there nonetheless remains a residue of the old image in the prophets. It functions not only as a source of nostalgia, the wistful recollection of what their life could have been, but also as a real and continuing option for what their life could yet be. The thought keeps returning that the disruptiveness caused by their prophetic vocation could be healed by simply turning their backs on it, by returning, that is, to the path their life was treading on before the call of God intervened. There is a tremendous seduction, after all, in domesticity, in leading a "home;' life (*domus*, home) that has become comfortable in the casual familiarity of its experiences. The prophets are not exempt from this seduction. Their vocation does not blot out anything of what they once were, whether of their sin (and hence their fear of hypocrisy in preaching God's will) or of their dreams and hopes (and hence their perception of the disruptiveness now present in their life). In each case it takes little sympathy to understand why the prophet engages the prophetic life with reluctance.

Who can see clearly into the soul of another human being? Who can see what untempered feelings are driving another's life, the passions that give it a sense of purpose and meaning? The only way we can discover the answer is by observing the life itself, the way the individual's activity articulates what is going on inside. Jesus said as much when he offered his own criterion for gaining knowledge of other people: "By their fruits you shall know them." It is what an individual *in fact* does, whether or not wanting to do it, whether or not reluctant to do it, that provides the standard for our judgment of him or her.

This is the same standard, then, that we bring to our judgment of the prophets, and all those who would lead a prophetic life. Their reluctance to engage their vocation does not tell us that the vocation has been half-heartedly pursued; it only tells us that they are human, with fears and desires. How their vocation has been pursued, rather, must be determined not on the basis of what is happening within them (anything can be happening there) but on the basis of what is happening outside them, that is, on the basis of what they do. And there we see, despite all their reluctance, a single-minded, enthusiastic commitment to doing the will of God they have been called to.

The prophet, in short, can never be understood within the pastel piety of the quietist, the individual who does nothing but wait for God's will to be revealed in all the given situations of life. For the prophet, God's will is already known, and there is no need for further waiting but only for action, for *doing* what the will reveals. It is this need to act, to enflesh in deeds what God has spoken, that gives us our fundamental indication of the prophet's enthusiasm, that "in-Godness" that sets him or her apart from the quietist who always claims a ready desire to do God's will but never seems quite certain what it is.

Finally, and obviously, this latter attitude is especially disastrous for a Christian since it ignores or diminishes in importance the clarity and sufficiency of God's will manifest in the life of Jesus, and so destroys the possibility of a truly prophetic, a passionate response to the call Jesus cries to all who would be his disciples.

WILLINGNESS AS A WAY OF LIFE

In dreams and fantasies we may delight in seeing ourselves as independent, "without ties" as the saying goes. We may picture ourselves as pleasurably autonomous, free to think and be whatever we wish, whenever we choose. We may fancy ourselves blind to the concerns of others before us, indifferent to their demands or needs, untouched even by their very existence. They have nothing to offer or take from us, we imagine; we are sufficient unto ourselves. In these dreams and fantasies we resurrect in our lives the spirit of Narcissus, the "comeliest of youths" described in Ovid's great poem, *The Metamorphoses*.

Narcissus is the paradigm of the complete egomaniac. He is someone who thinks the center of his life contains only one inhabitant, himself, and that all others are therefore peripheral, expendable "props" that he employs to fulfill his wants. He would never think, for example, of turning his eyes from himself toward the heavens, pondering the beauty of the stars as a limitless source of wonder. For if he did he would at once know his immense insignificance in the order of creation. He would know that the stars outstrip him in comeliness and their magnitude makes a mockery of his sense of self-esteem. The heavens would teach him the meaning of humility and powerlessness, the strange peace that comes from knowing that creation would be as wondrous had he never lived, and that his life is therefore a blessing. He would be able to see beneath his self-esteem, into himself and his own insignificance, and laugh; and beyond it, into the heavens and the world of other persons, and be thankful. But no, all directions in the geography of Narcissus's life eventually lead back to himself, and he finds this enormously satisfying. The psychological terrain in which he exists is that of an untempered self-indulgence wherein the only criterion for behavior is the pleasure associated with always "having one's way."

Yet, such dreams are only that: dreams, fancies, imaginings. They are delicate constructs in a wistful world where we are the creator and director of all that takes place. They are woven from the conceit we are all capable of and which courses through our life like the holding threads in a tapestry. Like all dreams, they shatter upon awakening and their unreality becomes plain. We realize that we are not completely autonomous but also dependent; that our world is not all our own but also shared; and that before us there are others we must interact with if we are ever to become the selves we hope to be. We realize, in short, that Narcissus is a fiction; that he might exist in imagination but can never exist in reality. Above all his protests, then, that he is an island unto himself there is heard the ringing contradiction of the great poet: No man is an island entire of itself.

These words, not the protests of Narcissus, ring true as soon as we hear them. They have provided a guiding spirit for our reflections in this book because they sound a fundamental lesson of every prophet, that we acknowledge and learn to appreciate the fact that there is Power in our lives that we cannot control, that it shapes the meaning of what we are and will be, and that it takes the form of God and other people.

The song Narcissus sings is one to his own glory, a hymn of self-praise claiming his role as creator of his world, master of all that moves about him, and arbiter of his values. But the song of the prophet, like the psalms of the Old Testament, is sung to the glory of God. It is a hymn of praise to the giver of life, the guide of creation's course, and the revealer of right and wrong. And it is a hymn of thankfulness as well that the prophet is not alone but shares with others the gifts of life, the created world, and the knowledge of right and wrong. Narcissus can sing only of himself; the prophet sings only of others.

When you first meet a stranger, or a friend not seen for a while, the first gesture you make is normally an outreaching one, the handshake or embrace. The gesture is a symbol, of your willingness to take the stranger or friend into your life and make him or her feel welcome there. It is to say in a specific action, "I greet you; I am at your disposal; I am willing to make you a part of me so that we might enjoy and even learn from each other's presence." Only when the individual before us is somehow perceived as a threat will we hesitate in our gesture of welcome. Only when we suspect that the stranger might disrupt our lives in ways we fear will we be unwilling to converse with him or her. Only when we think he or she will enter our lives and make demands we wish to avoid will we be reluctant to extend our hand or embrace with inviting grace. Instead, we will hold back, constructing a barrier that the other will now breach only when he or she proves our fears and suspicions misguided.

Such a handshake or embrace is not a perfunctory, empty gesture, as it often is in our every day lives. It is not like the ritual morning kiss between a husband and wife whose love changed years ago into mere tolerance, or the pat on the back between athletes who in fact are bitter rivals. Here it is much, much more. It is a confession that at least for the time being we are muffling the spirit of Narcissus that roams our minds and hearts. The contact of bodies in the handshake or embrace indicates the contact between selves that we wish to initiate or renew. The contact eliminates the separation between us, the autonomy of our separate selves. The words the other speaks to us we will now hear with enthusiasm, an attentiveness born of the desire to communicate. What we are doing with our gesture, in other words, is recognizing (as Heidegger describes it) that language is the shepherd of being. We are acknowledging that for a relationship to exist between us, for a community of being to occur that is more than I and more than you — a community that is *we* — language must be spoken. The gesture is the invitation we offer each other to initiate this speaking, and so to establish our community. Or metaphorically expressed: It is only the first movement in a dance that is completed by language. Left alone, frozen in space and time without the following movement of language, the gesture thus becomes as meaningless and grotesque, as uncomfortable and embarrassing, even painful, as an arabesque stopped in mid-step.

An enduring, devoted silence will always kill human relationships. Silence slowly squeezes the breath out of love and friendship while it feeds contempt and indifference to vigorous health. That is why the hurt that lovers inflict on each other never becomes quite so exquisite as when it takes the form of the refusal to speak to each other. Perhaps better than describing it as the shepherd of being, then, we should describe language as the mid-wife of our emotions, just as it is of our logic. Without it our passions would be fruitless, just as our logic would be stillborn. In some fashion, by gestures and words, we must communicate with each other in receptive ways if our relationships are to survive. Or else, as we said at the close of the preceding chapter, we consign ourselves to the hellish existence of a lonely individualism. When others call to us, when they beckon toward us in a way that is inviting us into their life, human community is served only when we accept the invitation. Refusal to do so will always place the possiblity of this community in immediate peril, and then begin to unmuffle within us the spirit of Narcissus.

It is true, of course, that our relationships with others always hold an element of chance. Even when we think we know others well, and that our anticipations of their behavior are fair and well-advised, there still remains the possibility that our availibility to them will be misused. We cannot be naive about this point, though most of us, I suspect, have already experienced its truth sufficiently enough in our lives. Whenever we reach out to others, and by our gestures and words seek to create communion with them, we make disappointments, frustrations, spoiled hopes accessible experiences. But before the possibility of these experiences we cannot blind ourselves to the equal possibility that our communion with others might also be a continual source of wisdom, peace, and blessing, and that this possibility is worth any chance we might take of its not occurring.

What we have been describing in these several paragraphs is what we have been describing throughout this book as the *willingness* that characterizes the prophet's life. Even when it is shaded by reluctance, this willingness is never overcome, so that when relating to others it means what the handshake or embrace does when you greet someone. It is the recognition that you must go out to the other, placing yourself at his or her disposal.

When the other is someone in need, prophetic willingness means practicing the self-abandonment that allows you to dispossess yourself of what you have (or can gain) in order to meet this need. When the other is your God, prophetic willingness means practicing the self-abandonment that allows you to become powerless, to seek not your will, your own desires and designs for life, but God's. In both instances prophetic willingness involves the recognition that the other is before us, God and neighbor, to be approached and embraced, not held at a distance. In both cases it requires the poverty of spirit Jesus taught and blessed in his sermon on the mount, the willingness to give of oneself completely to the service of others, to hand over one's life to their needs.

Webster defines reluctance as "the state of struggling against; resistance." What every true prophet knows is that a point is finally reached when struggle against a vocation must be abandoned and one must yield to the guidance it will give one's life. For until that happens a vocation cannot exercise its full claim on an individual and he or she will not fully understand what it means to be committed to a task. The noble mind knows when its limits have been reached, its excuses have run out, and it is time to submit. It knows there can be no grace in struggle, no virtue in resistence, no worth in reluctance when this nobility is offended and we refuse to submit simply from pride or fear. Then we create a barrier between ourself and our tasks that proves our blindness to the meaning of prophetic willingness. And when these tasks involve the will of God and needs of others, we prove ourself *reprehensibly* blind to this meaning. For the tasks of the prophetic life, as we have said throughout this book, are never simply a bald option for the prophet, something he or she may or may not do with equal effect. Rather, they are a *responsibility* in the most elemental sense of the word. They establish a pattern of behavior in life the prophet *must respond* to if he or she is to exercise at all the integrity required of a prophetic vocation.

I do not make this point on my own, without guidance or support. For it is the very same point that Jesus himself makes when, like us, he identifies both the primary objects of the prophet's concern — God and neighbor — and the primary motive that impels the prophet's activity. When confronted by his disciples with the question of which were the most important of God's commands, Jesus says, "The first command is this: Love God with all your heart and mind and soul. And the second is like the first: Love your neighbor as you love yourself. In these two commands all the law and prophets are fulfilled" (Matthew 22:37-40).

The other person before us always stands waiting: To be embraced not at all; or to be embraced, only to be let go; or to be embraced eternally, forever a part of what we ourselves are. We must make the decision: Shall the other be nothing to us; or something to us; or everything to us? The reflections in this book are concerned with just this type of question, easily posed but difficult to answer. Yet the most they can do is to help the reader, one way or another, in answering it. They cannot by themselves provide the answer, which must finally come from each individual alone. And always:

There is the other, God and the neighbor, awaiting our decision, awaiting the gift of our prophetic willingness, our self-abandoned love.

QUESTIONS FOR REFLECTION AND DISCUSSION

1. We spoke of conscience in this chapter. Is conscience the final arbiter of what is right and wrong for an individual?

2. Belief in demons is a commonplace among the biblical prophets — for example, the false prophet we described in this chapter (and elsewhere in the book) is frequently understood as demon-possessed. Do you believe in the existence of unseen, independent powers of evil in the world?

3. Do we have an obligation to criticize others for the same faults we ourselves are guilty of?

4. In the prophetic view, domesticity (living in a comfortable rut or routine) is a very great temptation, one to which most human beings succumb even when they believe they have been called by God to live differently. What do you think of domesticity?

5. How would you respond to the prophetic question about death, which is not so much, "Is there life after death?" but rather, "Is there something I am willing to die for?"

Christian Commitment and Prophetic Living

Our century has witnessed more changes in patterns of thinking and acting — in behavioral ideals — than perhaps any single century preceding it. It is an era of great technological advances, affecting not only the sciences but all areas of human endeavor. It is an era of speed, not waiting for the hesitant and doubtful. It is an era of complexity, expanding and complicating the tasks that individuals undertake, and regarding simplicity as tantamount to simple-mindedness. In whatever direction we turn, it seems we are forced to re-examine our values, whether religious, philosophical, social, political, or economic. Many of us, too, are no longer at ease resigning ourselves to a life of seclusion, immune to the influences of the world around us and satisfied to accept age-old visions of the purpose and meaning of life. We live in an era that is eroding the foundations of long established institutions, that is enlarging the range of human encounters, and that in many instances is replacing traditional concepts of God with the realities of science.

Ideas and values can no longer be easily dictated to us. We must arrive at them ourselves.

Yet we are not as far removed from our ancestors as we might think. For like them we still ask questions about the meaning of life, and still seek to identify commitments for ourselves that will provide this meaning. Yet, our questions and answers are surely no more perplexing or satisfying than the similar questions and answers of our forebears. Starting as far back as Gilgamesh, eighteen hundred years before Homer, humans have recorded the way they have looked at their lives, questioned its significance, and sought commitments to give it meaning. Though approached differently at various times by various men and women, these concerns are thus neither exclusive nor more urgent to our own or any age.

What all this really means, of course, is that there has never been any final solution to the question of life's meaning that compels universal acceptance. Rather, we have always sought and will always continue to seek commitments to drive our existence, allowing us to formulate approaches to the needs within us and the world around us whereby life itself can become, if not completely understandable, at least more acceptable. And if in this search we eventually come to judge some commitments as foolish or misdirected, it is only because we have been disciplined (or fortunate) enough to have found commitments of our own that satisfy us, but which, on an objective appraisal, we also know do not forbid the possibility of others emerging in our lives.

If we are Christians there can be only one fundamental commitment that drives our life: to become Christ-like. Should we lose sight of this commitment, then, our very reason for living goes blind. We start wandering, now here, now there, toward different goals that prove our professed commitment to becoming Christ-like a sham, or a pity. Our life becomes kaleidoscopic, with its patterns of meaning shifting simultaneously with its goals, until we lose all sense of lasting direction to what we are doing and where we are going. At this point, however, any commitment we still profess as Christians must finally either die or raise itself to new life with reaffirmed strength and attentiveness.

But this living, strong, and attentive commitment every Christian is asked to profess — it has been our task throughout this book to demonstrate that it must involve the character of prophecy.

Christian life must be a prophetic life because Christ himself was a prophet. For all the gospels witness to his experience of a call (if only implicitly), an address by the Father to preach the Father's will. And they all witness to the authority this call gave him (to abrogate the old Law, to heal wounds, forgive sins, teach without compromise). And they all speak of the criticism he also engaged in (especailly of the Pharisees, but of his own disciples too) and his political involvement (particularly over the claims of his messiahship, his treatment during his trial and passion, and generally in the way his message proclaims the dignity, worth, and inviolateness of every individual in the sight of God). Finally, all the gospels tell of his reluctance to engage the tasks of the prophetic life he has been called to. We need only rehearse the scene in Gethsemane, its frightened prayers and requests, before the greatest of his lessons was taught — how to die.

Just as Christ led a prophetic life, then, so must we, if we are committed to becoming Christ-like. For only then will our commitment, despite all the conflicts and joys it may involve, be true and firm and open-eyed. Only then will we see, and in seing be able to approach the more closely, the goal of all Christian living, the time of the Father's blessing when we can say, "I live now not with my own life but with the life of Christ who lives in me" (Galatians 2:20).

Let me conclude this book by recalling that throughout these pages we have noticed in a variety of ways the prophetic awareness that in any fruitful human encounter that brings individuals together in their common experiences there is more than me involved, more than you, and more than the mere sum of me and you. The unity that is achieved, the word or action that unites us, is in some way before, between, and ahead of us. Neither I nor you can produce it or compel it to come into being. It happens of its own accord, somewhat like a wonder, somewhat like a gift, but always beyond our total control. If we call this power that unites us and gives us the wondrous possibility to understand and become one with each other by the name of God, then our common striving for God means that God is neither totally beyond our existence nor only indifferently involved with it.

In this way, to understand the many possible views of God as somehow proving that God does not exist would be a complete misunderstanding of what it means to have faith in God. Not only that, it would also be the mistaken boast that one has seen God face to face, and in seeing him has seen nothing. For God is as much a part of us, and as much a mystery to us, as our own untempered feelings for life, for love, for peace: God is a Power working in and for us in the past, the present, and toward the future. To be sure, the contradictions of life, the divorce between our desires for happiness and repose and an irrational world that constantly obstructs them can result from one viewpoint in an absurd vision of life and the world. But from a different viewpoint, they can also be the catalysts for a vibrant faith in which the conviction of the finite absurdity of the world and one's life give way to the possibility that Christ's awesome message of power over life is true. Then the inadequacy of self-sufficiency is replaced by the possibility that a sympathetic identity with Jesus can alone fulfill our desires for self-realization, converse with God, and immortal joy.

Bibliography

Anderson, Bernhard W., and Walter Harrelson, eds. *Israel's Prophetic Heritage.* New York: Harper & Row, 1962.

Bright, John. *Jeremiah,* Anchor Bible. New York: Doubleday & Company, 1965.

Buber, Martin. *The Prophetic Faith,* C. Witton-Davies, trans. New York: Macmillan, 1949.

Clements, R.E. *Prophecy and Covenant.* London: S. C. M. Press, 1965.

_____. *Prophecy and Tradition.* Atlanta: John Knox Press, 1975.

Crenshaw, James L. *Prophetic Conflict: Its Effect Upon Israelite Religion.* Berlin/New York: Walter de Gruyter, 1971.

DeVries, Simon John. *Prophet Against Prophet.* Grand Rapids, Mi: William B. Eerdmans, 1978.

Gottwald, Norman K. *All the Kingdoms of the Earth: Israelite Prophecy and International Realtions in the Ancient Near East.* New York: Harper & Row, 1964.

Heaton, E.W. *The Old Testament Prophets.* Atlanta: John Knox Press, 1977.

Henshaw, Thomas. *The Latter Prophets.* London: Allen & George Unwin Ltd., 1958.

Heschel, Abraham J. *The Prophets.* New York: Harper & Row, 1963.

Johnson, Aubrey R. *The Cultic Prophet in Ancient Israel.* Cardiff: University of Wales, 1961.

Koch, Klaus. *The Growth of the Biblical Tradition,* S.M. Cupitt, trans. New York: Charles Scribner's Sons, 1969.

Kuhl, Curt. *The Prophets of Israel.* London: Oliver & Boyd, 1960.

Lindblom, J. *Prophecy in Ancient Israel*. Oxford: Basil Blackwell, 1962.

McKane, William. *Prophets and Wise Men*, Studies in Biblical Theology. Napierville, Il: Alex R. Allenson, 1965.

Orlinsky, Harry M., ed. *Interpreting the Prophetic Tradition*, The Goldensen Lectures 1955-1966. Cincinnati: The Hebrew Union College Press, 1969.

Overholt, Thomas W. *The Threat of Falsehood: A Study in the Theology of the Book of Jeremiah*, Studies in Biblical Theology, 2nd series, no. 16. London: S. C. M. Press, 1970.

Rad, Gerhard, von. *Old Testament Theology*, Vol. II, D. M. G. Stalker, trans. New York: Harper & Row, 1965.

Scott, R. B. Y. *The Relevance of the Prophets*, rev. ed. New York: Macmillan, 1976.

Skinner, John. *Prophecy and Religion*. New York: Cambridge University Press, 1922.

Westermann, Claus. *Basic Forms of Prophetic Speech*, Hugh K. White, trans. Philadelphia: The Westminster Press, 1967.

Winward, Stephen. *A Guide to the Prophets*. Atlanta: John Knox Press, 1976.